QUIN SHERRER & RUTHANNE GARLOCK

A *Woman's* Guide to
SPIRITUAL
WARFARE

Protect Your Home, Family and Friends from Spiritual Darkness

Regal

From Gospel Light
Ventura, California, U.S.A.

Published by Regal
From Gospel Light
Ventura, California, U.S.A.
www.regalbooks.com
Printed in the U.S.A.

The circumstances of certain events and some names of persons and locations
have been changed to protect individuals' privacy.

Library of Congress Cataloging-in-Publication Data
The Library of Congress has catalogued the first edition as follows:
Sherrer, Quin.
A Woman's guide to spiritual warfare : a woman's guide for battle / Quin Sherrer
and Ruthanne Garlock.
p. cm.
Includes bibliographical references and index.
ISBN 978-08307-4748-1
1. Women—Religious life. I. Garlock, Ruthanne. II. Title.
BV4527.S43 1991
248.8'43—dc20
91-3837
CIP

1 2 3 4 5 6 7 8 9 10 / 15 14 13 12 11 10

Rights for publishing this book outside the U.S.A. or in non-English languages are
administered by Gospel Light Worldwide, an international not-for-profit ministry.
For additional information, please visit www.glww.org, email info@glww.org, or write to
Gospel Light Worldwide, 1957 Eastman Avenue, Ventura, CA 93003, U.S.A.

A Woman's Guide to Spiritual Warfare

Contents

ACKNOWLEDGMENTS

Thanks to all those who prayed for us while this project and its revision were underway.

Thanks also to all the women who willingly allowed us to share their stories—defeats as well as victories. Without your transparency our job would have been impossible.

Special gratitude and love to the Lord Jesus Christ, our Commander in Chief, who calls us, equips us and goes ahead of us into battle; and to the Holy Spirit, our faithful Guide.

INTRODUCTION

Soon after this book was first released in 1991, it hit the top-selling list for Christian books in the spiritual-warfare category. In fact, it kept that rating for six years, and both men and women were reading it as a classic on the topic.

When our friend Ann Spangler (then senior editor at Servant Publications) first asked us to take on the project, I (Quin) immediately said, "No, I don't want to pay the price to write on that topic." But Ruthanne talked me into it just before she left on a ministry trip to Africa.

What have I committed to? I kept wondering. But as we began to write, both of us became transparent in our own struggles, and it was a great learning experience for us. We interviewed dozens of women who had successfully found victory, and they readily shared their scriptural strategies and insights. We also gained a new appreciation for the many prayer partners who faithfully prayed for us during the process.

Now, almost 20 years later, many of those same prayer partners are still praying for us. And we continue to receive testimonies from folks whose lives were changed by the principles they learned from reading this book.

Once, I (Quin) was on a flight from Orlando to Atlanta when I introduced myself to the young woman sitting beside me. As soon as I mentioned my name, she literally screamed, "You wrote that book! That book saved my marriage and my children—*A Woman's Guide to Spiritual Warfare*! I copied the prayers in it and asked my husband to pray them aloud with me every day. Our daughter was falling into bad company, but we used those prayers and examples to give us hope. Today we are a family following the Lord."

My new friend spent the rest of the trip sharing examples of how she used the prayers from the book and how their family became active in a church. She even corresponded with me for a while.

The other day a friend called me from Virginia. "Just wanted you to know I minister in a prison here," she said. "A woman I was talking to about the Lord was reading your book—behind bars yet!—and said it was really helping her."

I (Ruthanne) have had countless similar encounters with women who have told me that reading the book and praying the prayers in it saved their marriage, healed a broken relationship with a prodigal child, or helped them break free from bondage.

For several years running, one woman would come to my book table every summer at the annual gathering for my ministry fellowship group. She would buy five or six copies of the book to give to the military wives she was mentoring in prayer and spiritual warfare. Just recently another friend told me that she keeps a copy of the book on her bedside table so she can refer to it often. It seems many readers not only keep their own book handy for frequent reference, but they also buy copies to give away. Many times after I've spoken at a meeting, one or more women would buy the book off my table and ask me to sign it, saying, "I had this book and loaned it out but never got it back. I have to have another one!"

Although we don't claim to be experts on the subject, we have gained some knowledge about spiritual warfare through our research and study and through our own times "in the trenches." This revision of our classic book is an accumulation of our combined experience and of testimonies from women just like you who are learning to be skilled warriors.

Through this practical handbook, we aim to help women understand the *why* and the *how* of spiritual warfare, based on biblical examples and contemporary experiences. In these pages, we will address many questions:

- What is spiritual warfare?
- Is there a scriptural mandate for spiritual warfare?
- Who is the enemy, and who started the war?
- Is warfare only for specialists?
- Is there a cost to ignoring this war?
- What weapons are we to use?
- Is every mishap from Satan?
- If Jesus won the victory, why do we have to fight?
- Isn't it enough simply to pray and leave the outcome in God's hands?
- What about the battle in the mind?
- How can we distinguish between God's voice and the enemy's voice?
- How is Satan working in women's lives today?
- How do we become vulnerable to his work?
- How can we feel secure against his attacks?
- What should we do when we become battle weary?

As we share answers to these questions and recount experiences to illustrate them, you will gain insight and confidence about fighting your own spiritual battles. Also, you'll be able to encourage and strengthen a friend who may be suffering an enemy attack.

Why a spiritual warfare book for women? Aren't men also called to duty? Yes, of course they are. But we believe women have a special interest in this battle. After all, our involvement in the war began with the woman and the serpent in the Garden of Eden. And it's the seed of the woman—Jesus—who has bruised the head of the serpent and secured the enemy's defeat.

We believe spiritual warfare is of special interest to women for these reasons:

- Women tend to be more sensitive to the spiritual realm than men—including the area of occult activity—but their sensitivity should be guided by the Holy Spirit.

• Women can become competent spiritual warriors—especially for those they love—because of their loyalty in relationships.

• Today's women face unique difficulties that need to be addressed in the context of spiritual warfare: single parenting, troubled marriages, careers, the "super mom" syndrome, media influence, coping with addicted children and spouses, abortion, materialism, financial pressures— the list goes on and on.

We feel these problems can be better addressed by praying and waging spiritual warfare against Satan's schemes rather than by relying solely on protests or demonstrations to achieve social and political change. Our purpose is best expressed by the motto adopted by Moravian missionaries to the Caribbean in the 1700s: "To gain for the Lamb the reward of His sacrifice."

Be assured that Jesus has done everything necessary to ensure our victory over Satan, but that does not mean it's a walkover, as our battle scars confirm. Yes, Christ came to set the captives free, but all the prisoners haven't yet heard the good news. So we must be faithful to the call to spiritual combat.

Whether you are a seasoned prayer warrior or a new volunteer, this book is for you. It will bring encouragement, hope and strategies, and also help you gain new Scripture ammunition for your prayer arsenal.

Both conventional war and spiritual warfare are expensive, requiring discipline, dedication, tears and travail—in some cases even lives, as Church history reveals. But to have a part in the ultimate victory and hear Jesus say, "Well done, good and faithful servant," is worth the battle.

We invite you to turn the page and embark upon your new prayer journey.

—Quin Sherrer and Ruthanne Garlock

A *Woman's* Guide to
SPIRITUAL
WARFARE

But I Never Wanted to Be in a Battle!

For our struggle is not against flesh and blood, but against the rulers, against the authorities, against the powers of this dark world and against the spiritual forces of evil in the heavenly realms.

EPHESIANS 6:12

"I resist you in the name of Jesus and command you to go!" Claudia said with a quavering voice. To her amazement, the hideous black leopard turned and ran. Startled, she awoke from the bad dream and sat up in bed. "I realized the Lord was teaching me in my dream to do spiritual warfare—that the name of Jesus really has power," shared this trim brunette. "I had accepted Jesus as my Savior and Lord and had received the Holy Spirit. But then my mind was bombarded with fear and condemnation. I loved God more than anything, yet the enemy made me think I had blasphemed the Holy Spirit and would never be able to please God."

Claudia had never received any teaching on how to deal with fear. She had heard some comments about spiritual warfare but had no clue as to what that meant. She thought she simply had to endure this struggle in exchange for her salvation. Then came her dream.

"In the dream, I was constantly being pursued by a huge black leopard," she said. "I pushed it out the door and it came in the window. Everywhere I went it followed me. I was terrified. Then I sensed the Lord say to me, 'Claudia, resist the leopard in the name of Jesus.' In my dream I stopped running, turned and faced the leopard, and commanded it to leave in Jesus' name. I was happily surprised to see it flee!"

Claudia's friend Jean took her to a woman who ministers in deliverance, because there was witchcraft in Claudia's family background, and she had used drugs in college. The Lord broke these and many related bondages.

Jean became Claudia's prayer partner and began training her in scriptural truths. "Now," Claudia says, "I know a Christian can truly be victorious over the spiritual forces of evil that Paul talks about in Ephesians."

Do We Need to Fight the Devil?

My (Quin's) subject was prayer. My audience, three-dozen pastors' wives. I had been asked to teach a weekend workshop at a rustic lodge hidden away in the Georgia pines. But after the first session, during which I had briefly discussed spiritual warfare, the leader who had invited me knocked on my door.

"Quin, you've offended some of our women here," she said apologetically. "Several of them have PhDs, and they don't believe Christians need to fight the devil in our day and age. Please tone down your message."

I had only shared some basic guidelines on intercession and how to pray the Word of God as a means of opposing the enemy. Then I had explained that Satan—not another person—is our enemy, and we need to be on guard against his tactics. I was stunned to think a group of pastors' wives would find such teaching offensive. But I agreed to adapt my material.

The apostle Paul's many references to spiritual warfare clearly indicate that he considered battling against the powers of darkness to be normal activity for Christians. But my experience at the retreat offers a graphic example of a common attitude among many Christians today.

"Spiritual warfare? Those two words don't go together!" one friend exclaimed upon hearing of plans for this book.

We might ask these people, "Don't you even believe the devil exists?" Well, yes, they do—"theologically speaking." But the tendency is to think of Satan not as a personality or a being who affects us directly, but simply as a pervasive influence of evil in the world.

In fact, a Barna Group survey states that 4 out of 10 Christians (40 percent) strongly agreed that Satan "is not a living being but is a symbol of evil," while only about 30 percent of Christians indicated that they believe Satan is real. Some were honest enough to say they weren't sure what they believe about the existence of Satan. Regarding the survey, George Barna said:

> Most Americans, even those who say they are Christian, have doubts about the intrusion of the supernatural into the natural world. Hollywood has made evil accessible and tame, making Satan and demons less worrisome than the Bible suggests they really are. It's hard for achievement-driven, self-reliant, independent people to believe that their lives can be impacted by unseen forces.[1]

C. S. Lewis wisely wrote, "There are two equal and opposite errors into which our race can fall about the devils. One is to disbelieve in their existence. The other is to believe, and to feel an excessive and unhealthy interest in them."[2]

Some of the pastors' wives at that retreat had apparently fallen into the first error. Either they didn't believe in Satan's existence, or they mistakenly felt there was nothing they should be doing about it.

"Maybe the next time one of these women faces a direct attack from the enemy in her life, she'll think about what I said," I told my prayer partner who had accompanied me to the retreat. "Well, you gave them the Word of God," my friend assured me. "And His Word never returns void."

The next afternoon as we were packing my car to leave, a young pastor's wife ran up to me. "I just want you to know that your first lesson really opened my eyes," she said exuberantly. "I'm going home to apply some of those spiritual warfare methods, and I know things are going to change! I now realize my rebellious teenage son is not the enemy. I intend to use Scripture as a weapon to fight the devil, just as you showed us."

Deborah's Example

The biblical Deborah challenges us to lay aside some of our own worthy interests and activities to deal with the spiritual battles at hand. We read of Deborah, a prophetess and judge in Israel, in the fourth chapter of Judges. She held court under a palm tree between Bethel and Ramah at a time when Israel was suffering bitter oppression under Jabin, a Canaanite king who had defeated Israel and occupied its land.

The name "Jabin" means "cunning," and the Canaanite word comes from a root word meaning "to humiliate or bring under subjection." Deborah must have heard daily reports of Jabin's cruel treatment. His army general, Sisera, constantly terrorized the people with his nine hundred chariots of iron, while Israel's army had almost no weapons for their defense. No doubt Deborah became increasingly incensed over the situation and joined the people of Israel in crying out to the Lord for deliverance.

We modern Deborahs need to feel that same indignation about Satan's work. By engaging in prayer and spiritual warfare, we can take a stand against the enemy's oppression in our own world.

The enemy works in many ways today—some more subtle than others. It seems his iron chariots come in all sizes! Perhaps you recognize yourself in one or more of these everyday attacks, which a friend calls household sins:

- Strife and disharmony too often disrupt your family relationships.
- Someone you love has been unjustly treated by another Christian; you take up the defense and find yourself becoming bitter and cynical.
- Your anger seems to erupt at the slightest provocation.
- You suffer with guilt because you don't feel you're a very successful Christian.
- You struggle with envy when comparing your own circumstances with your friends' seemingly carefree lives.
- Insecurity and anxiety over the future frequently overwhelm you.
- Your prayer life is inconsistent, and you often feel that your prayers bounce back in your face.

But I Don't Want to Fight!

A friend once said to me, "Quin, I never wanted to have to fight the devil. I just wanted to remain a normal Christian, go to church, mind my own business and not cause trouble!" But when her son got into drugs, she learned spiritual warfare out of necessity.

Thousands of women feel they've just been tending to "business as usual," trying their best to live a good Christian life. Suddenly an iron chariot comes roaring through their household, church, business or community, thrusting them into confrontation with the enemy. And they cry out, "Help!" You may be facing a battle similar to one of the following that women have shared with us:

- Your pregnant, unwed daughter is convinced that getting an abortion is the answer to her dilemma.

19

- You learn your child is on drugs, and the dealer has been attending the church youth group.
- You discover a cache of pornographic literature in your husband's closet.
- A teenage acquaintance confides that she was sexually abused by her father, who is a deacon in the church.
- An adult porn shop opens in your neighborhood, and local authorities seem totally indifferent to the situation.
- Your teenager goes into rebellion, gets caught up in rock music and runs away from home to join a satanist group.
- A widow you and your husband befriended convinces him that it is God's will for him to divorce you and marry her.

Such situations actually confront many Christian women today—women whose eyes are opening to the spiritual battle they are already in, even though they feel unprepared. No longer do they need to be persuaded that a war is on. They are looking for guidance as to how to fight the battle!

Deborah Acted on God's Promise

We can learn more from Deborah about how to deal with spiritual enemies. After suffering 20 long years of Jabin's oppression, the people of Israel began to beseech God for deliverance. He responded by instructing Deborah to say to Barak, the general of Israel's army: "The LORD, the God of Israel, commands you: 'Go take with you ten thousand men of Naphtali and Zebulun and lead the way to Mount Tabor. I will lure Sisera, the commander of Jabin's army, with his chariots and his troops to the Kishon River and give him into your hands'" (Judg. 4:6-7).

Barak, who had faced this formidable enemy before, was fearful—and with good cause. A weak volunteer army with no chariots and few weapons was no match for Sisera's well-trained army of a hundred thousand men![3] But Barak was assessing the situation strictly from a logistics point of view. <u>Facts and truth are not always the same!</u> The truth was that God had promised victory in spite of the odds, if Israel would obey Him. Deborah—who was called "a mother in Israel" (Judg. 5:7)—was willing to stake the nation's future on that promise. What courage it took to give such bold instructions to Israel's army general! But <u>she acted on God's truth, not on the circumstantial fac</u>t that the Israelites were outnumbered by their enemy.

Barak agreed to go but only if Deborah went with him. After all, she was the one with the word from God. So in order to see her people liberated, Deborah assumed the role of a military commander to accompany Barak in leading the troops to battle (see Judg. 4:8-10). It was a necessary but unpleasant task.

God's Strategy

Deborah received specific orders from God about where Israel's troops were to be placed: Mount Tabor. As they approached the Kishon River, Sisera received intelligence reports as to Israel's movements. He gathered his army and went out against Israel, unaware that he was actually cooperating with God's plan.

This was the greatest display of Sisera's military might Barak and Deborah had ever seen. He had mobilized all his soldiers, weapons and chariots to annihilate Israel's weak army. Barak, surveying the situation from his vantage point on the mountain, may have had second thoughts about going into battle against Sisera. But Deborah was not deterred by this show of strength. She knew it was Sisera's *last* show!

As Sisera's army came close to the Kishon River, Bible scholars suggest that God caused a freak rainstorm, which blinded the soldiers and caused the river to flood, sweeping the iron chariots downstream (see Judg. 5:4,20-22). The name "Kishon" is from a root word meaning "to ensnare." Scripture records the outcome:

Then Deborah said to Barak, "Go! This is the day the LORD has given Sisera into your hands. Has not the LORD gone ahead of you?" So Barak went down Mount Tabor, followed by ten thousand men. At Barak's advance, the LORD routed Sisera and all his chariots and army by the sword, and Sisera abandoned his chariot and fled on foot. . . . All the troops of Sisera fell by the sword; not a man was left (Judg. 4:14-16).

One version of the text says, "Then the Lord threw the enemy into a panic. . . . Not one man was left alive" (Judg. 4:15-16, *TLB*).

Sisera took refuge in the tent of Jael, a Canaanite woman whom he thought he could trust. But Jael, choosing to align herself with the people of God, was not content to be a passive bystander in this war. Using household tools at hand—a mallet and a tent stake—she killed the enemy commander. End of Sisera. End of those dreaded iron chariots.

Amazing, isn't it? Two women were the key players in this drama in which God enabled a weak army, outnumbered ten to one, to win a resounding victory. Seven penetrating words end the story: "Then the land had peace forty years" (Judg. 5:31).

Deborah's Keys to Victory

Deborah and Barak were assured of victory because they battled according to God's instructions. God would not do it for them without their effort, nor did He reveal the entire strategy in advance. They had to obey God without knowing all the reasons why. God determined the place of the battle and told them how many soldiers to take.

When Deborah and Barak obeyed, doing what was possible for them to do, God responded by doing the "impossible," which only He could do.

These same principles apply in the spiritual battles we face. Final success is assured, but we have to seek God's direction and put forth some effort in obedience. When we use Deborah's seven keys to victory in assaulting the enemy's iron chariots, we too can see our enemy defeated:

1. She recognized that it was a *spiritual* battle and that God was going ahead of her small army.
2. She obeyed God's instructions, trusting His strategy.
3. She did not focus on the seeming strength of the enemy.
4. She did not waver in her confidence in God's Word.
5. She refused to be deterred by her colleague's lack of spiritual vision.
6. She never compromised with the enemy.
7. She gave praise and glory to God for the victory.

Surprised by Spiritual Warfare

I (Quin) remember back in 1972 when an iron chariot rolled through the church my mom was attending after she retired in Destin, Florida.[4] While visiting her there, I reluctantly agreed to attend one of their small home prayer meetings that Friday night. I soon learned they had gathered to pray for Bill, a 31-year-old Air Force veteran who attended their church. He was dying of acute leukemia at a hospital in Mississippi.

The prayer leader told me the doctors had diagnosed Bill with the worst form of leukemia, with his bone marrow mass-producing cancerous blood cells too rapidly for chemotherapy to be effective. The medical experts believed Bill had reached the end of his fight, and they didn't expect him to live through the weekend.

The group began crying out for God to intervene, but such intense prayer was completely foreign to me in those days. Not knowing how to participate, I told the Lord to "count me out." I didn't know whether He still healed or not; but if He did, I asked Him to hear the prayers of those gathered in this home, as they were praying with great faith and boldness.

One man shocked me when he began shouting, "Satan, we give you notice that you and your demonic forces cannot have Bill Lance. He is God's property, and we are standing in the gap for his complete healing. Spirits of infirmity, leave him, in Jesus' name." It was my first exposure to spiritual warfare.

These people really believe that Bill is going to be healed, I thought to myself. They told me that a few weeks earlier, the church had held a special healing service for him. As Bill knelt at the altar, Pastor Forrest Mobley and a group of elders had laid hands on him and had prayed that he would be healed. Here I was, a Christian at a home prayer meeting, unsure about the whole concept of healing for today, just looking on as this group battled for a man's life.

Later that same night, in the military hospital where he was being treated, Bill and his wife, Sharon, repeated the Lord's Prayer together in his room as they always did each night. Suddenly Bill began to sob. He later reported that he felt fire, like a charge of light, shooting through his body. Somehow he knew the presence of Jesus had filled the room.

The next morning, when doctors examined a bone marrow sample from his chest, there were no signs of cancerous cells. In fact, the sample was normal. Bill believed the hot light he had felt penetrating his body the night before had been God's healing touch flooding through him. You can imagine the joy those intercessors felt when they received the good report.

I have kept in touch with Bill since then, and after more than 35 years, I am glad to report that he is still well and very active. He told me on the phone a while back, "My career allows me to follow my passion and live a blessed life, as Sharon and I participate in church activities, and our children and grandchildren live nearby."

As for me, I no longer doubt that Jesus is our Healer. In fact, a year after Bill's healing, I wrote down his testimony and won a prestigious writing award, which actually launched me on my writing career and my understanding of spiritual warfare.

Yes, a woman's place is in the war! We recognize, as Deborah did, that God has gone ahead of us to defeat the enemy, but He wants us involved in the battle. And as Claudia discerned, we have authority in the name of Jesus.

Now let's take a closer look at our enemy.

Prayer

Thank You, Lord, for showing me that Satan is an enemy
who seeks to steal, kill and destroy Your purposes in my life.
Help me to learn from Deborah's example that as I put my
trust in You, I will receive strength and wisdom to fight my battles.
I praise You in advance for victories that will bring honor
and glory to Your name. Amen.

2

Who Is the Enemy, and What Does He Want from Me?

So the Lord said to the serpent . . . "I will put enmity between
you and the woman, and between your offspring and hers;
he will crush your head, and you will strike his heel."

GENESIS 3:14-15

Satan is our archenemy. Scripture clearly confirms that he's the foe of every human being, starting with Adam and Eve. The name "Satan" actually means "adversary, or one who opposes." Yet any discussion about warfare with this enemy tends to repel many believers.

"Satan, demons, evil principalities and powers—these are scary things that frighten people," some Christians say. "It's just too spooky!"

But to ignore this enemy and hope he will ignore us is both unrealistic and hazardous. Arthur Mathews says:

The terrifying fact of a hostile world of evil and malicious spirits paralyzes many Christians into inactivity and unwillingness to seek out biblical answers and to apply them. . . . There are many clear indications of Satan's motives and methods given us in the Bible, if only we would heed them. . . . His central purpose is to pull God from His throne in the minds of men and to take that throne himself.[1]

Why Satan Hates You and Me

Ever since God created Adam and Eve and placed them in the Garden of Eden, Satan has had a special hostility toward women. This fallen archangel, fuming with anger toward God and His creatures, lurked about the Garden, looking for a place where he could get a foothold and break the loving relationship between God and human beings.

Pride and rebellion led to Satan's own fall from heaven. Ultimately he induced Eve to succumb to those same sins. The serpent and the daughters of Eve have felt enmity ever since. Satan not only hated Eve, but he also hates all her offspring—including you and me.

This hatred was expressed centuries ago by the sacrifice of children to evil gods. Then at Jesus' birth, through King Herod's order to kill all the babies under age two, Satan tried to murder the Messiah. He failed. Later he engineered Jesus' crucifixion and thought he'd won at last. Actually, that was Satan's biggest mistake. Jesus' sacrificial death, burial and resurrection fulfilled the Father's plan to atone for sin and nullify Satan's plan. Scripture declares, "The reason the Son of God appeared was to destroy the devil's work" (1 John 3:8).

Godly women remain a frustration to Satan. Think about it! Women bring human beings into the world, and Satan hates humans. He still tries to do away with them through child sacrifice, abortion and sexual sin.

Blocking the Message

Jesus completed the work the Father gave Him to do on earth, and the enemy can do nothing to change that perfect plan of salvation.

But Satan *does* keep people from hearing the message; he also distorts and misrepresents the message. In other words, he vents his rage against the Father by taking vengeance on us. Satan tries to prevent our deliverance and keep us alienated from God, knowing this frustrates God's desire to see us reconciled to Himself.

Paul explains it: "If our gospel is veiled, it is veiled to those who are perishing. The god of this age has blinded the minds of unbelievers, so that they cannot see the light of the gospel of the glory of Christ, who is the image of God" (2 Cor. 4:3-4).

We then must oppose the spirits of darkness that blind and deceive the minds of the hearers. We must also resist evil forces trying to hinder our reaching people with the gospel. Our goal is to see men and women—believers and unbelievers—set free from the bondage of Satan by the power of the blood of Jesus.

Bible teacher Dean Sherman makes the point that God and Satan are not equally powerful forces standing in opposition to one another. Satan is merely a created being, while God is "the great uncreated Creator."[2] Speaking of Satan's attempt to exalt himself and become like God, Sherman says:

> What Satan did was absolutely ludicrous. Yet we, as finite, puny beings . . . think we can run our own lives without God. To try to live without God is to try to be God. This is exactly the absurd and insane pride that entered Satan's heart, and sadly, we all have it. . . . The being called Satan is merely a fallen archangel who received his name because he opposed God. He is also our adversary. We must consider him to be that—no more and no less.[3]

Binding Satan's Lie

Sue, a former student, called one day and asked me (Ruthanne) to pray for her unsaved father who had terminal cancer. Sue and her mother had prayed for years for him to accept Jesus. Now near death, he was very bitter, blaming God for his illness.

"How can we lead him to Christ when he is so angry?" Sue asked me.

"The problem is, he's believing Satan's lie that God is his enemy," I responded. "He needs to see that God is his only source of help. I suggest you bind the lying spirit that has deceived him. Then just shower your father with unconditional love; don't preach to him anymore."

Sue's mother and brother picked up extension phones, and I prayed while they agreed: "Thank You, Father, that it is Your desire to bring Sue's dad into Your kingdom. We take authority in the name of Jesus and bind the deceiving spirits that are lying to him. We ask the Holy Spirit to reveal the truth that You love him. Lord, cause him to come to his senses and escape from the trap of the devil. We ask this in Jesus' name, amen."

I suggested they continue this strategy. "Use the authority Jesus gave you to forbid the enemy to speak to your father."

About six weeks later, Sue called to tell me her father had died. But just before he died, he received Jesus as his Lord.

"One day as I walked through the living room where he was lying on the sofa, I went over and hugged him and said, 'I love you, Dad,'" Sue related. "Tears came to his eyes—it was the first time I had ever seen him cry. As I began to share with him about the Lord, I could tell that the Holy Spirit had already prepared his heart. He willingly accepted Jesus right then!"

This is a classic case of a person being deceived by evil spirits to believe God is his enemy. But his eyes were opened to the truth when spiritual warfare was done on his behalf. Realizing God truly was his friend, he repented.

How Does Satan Work?

We find in Scripture many names attributed to Satan and many descriptions of him, which reveal both his methods and his character:

- "crafty" (Gen. 3:1)
- "the deceiver" (Gen. 3:13)
- "the foe and the avenger" (Ps. 8:2)
- "the destroyer" (Isa. 54:16)
- "the tempter" (Matt. 4:3; 1 Thess. 3:5)
- "the evil one" (Matt. 6:13; John 17:15)
- "the ruler of the demons" [Beelzebub] (Matt. 12:24, *NKJV*)
- "a murderer" (John 8:44)
- "a liar and the father of lies" (John 8:44)
- "god of this age" (2 Cor. 4:4)
- "an angel of light" (2 Cor. 11:14)
- "the ruler of the kingdom of the air" (Eph. 2:2)
- "the dragon, . . . that ancient serpent" (Rev. 12:7-9)
- "the accuser" (Rev. 12:10).

Journalist and author McCandlish Phillips deftly describes the way Satan operates:

Consider the tactics of an enemy in battle. The enemy finds it far easier to send death upon his target if he conceals and hides his own position, so that he may strike by sudden surprise. Sneak attack, it is called. To obtain this advantage, the enemy moves in darkness, by stealth, and takes his position of advantage over the target in a hidden or camouflaged place. He wants the other side to be as unalert as possible, unguarded, unsuspecting, exposed to attack. The enemy will also use deceit and trickery to create a false impression of what and where the dangers are. The less the intended victims know of his existence, his position, his intention, and his power, the greater the advantage to him in bringing injury or death upon them.

These are the tactics of Satan toward man. The less you know about Satan, the better he likes it. Your ignorance of his tactics confers an advantage upon him, but he prefers that you do not even credit his existence. If you do not believe that he is, then you will do nothing to prepare yourself, or your family, or your children, against his activities, and by that neglect many are made his victims.[4]

The Enemy's Advantage

Several years ago I accompanied my husband, John Garlock, on a ministry trip to Guatemala. One day our host took us to the ancient city of Antigua to visit a historical museum. This region had once been inhabited by the Mayan Indians, but the Spanish conquered the area in the early 1500s. A huge mural in the museum depicts the conflict.

The Mayan Indians—who fought with bow and arrow—were known to be brave, fierce warriors. But the Spanish soldiers had a distinct advantage because they wore armor, and they had horses and guns. Horses were unknown in the Western Hemisphere at that time. So when the Indians saw one of these swift-footed animals with an armored soldier attached, they thought it was all one creature. They aimed at the horse, not realizing that the real enemy was the soldier astride the horse. Their arrows felled the horses in great numbers, but the armored soldiers jumped from their mounts and shot the Indians with their muskets.

The Mayans were massacred by the hundreds, and the Spanish easily seized control of the entire region.

"What a great illustration for spiritual warfare!" I exclaimed to my husband as we looked at the wall-to-wall painting. "The Indians were defeated because they failed to recognize the real enemy riding on the horse's back—and that's exactly what happens to countless Christians. They shoot at one another instead of fighting the devil."

"Well, then, " John responded, "when another person confronts us with meanness and malice, we'd better remind ourselves, 'He's not the enemy; he's only the horse!' " Perhaps a laughable analogy, but graphic nonetheless.

In many instances, Satan does his work unhindered simply because Christians are apathetic or too preoccupied to take notice. Edith Schaeffer says:

> There is a deafness, blindness, insensitivity of touch and feeling among many Christians who refuse to recognize the war in which *they* are involved, and who are spiritually "playing a violin" while the enemy attacks and scores victories unchallenged, given no resistance. . . . We are as stupid and negligent as any of the "Neros" who ever lived, if we simply entertain ourselves with Christian diversions and let ourselves and our children be attacked and devoured without entering into the army and setting up the defense we have been instructed to prepare.[5]

Satan Destroys Homes

One of the ways the enemy attacks women is by destroying their marriage, thus causing their children to grow up in a one-parent home. Psychologist Richard Dobbins reviews the damage Satan has done in this area:

> Out of the materialism of the 1950s, the narcissism of the 1960s, and the hedonism of the 1970s has risen a society that aborts its unborn, commercializes the care of its children, and warehouses its elderly. Blinded by such confused priorities, we are dehumanizing our country and destroying our family relationships. . . .
>
> Millions of broken families lie strewn across our land by a flagrant disregard for the sanctity of marriage and by selfishly sought divorces. Divorced mothers and their children comprise the largest group falling below the poverty line each year. Rising numbers of children in father-absent families are crippled in their search for a heterosexual identity.[6]

One of the Casualties

Rena, a pastor's daughter who grew up in church, fought hard for her 13-year marriage to Jack, her high-school sweetheart. She even resigned her position as minister of music at their church because he felt threatened by her being in the public eye. But he was "in love" with a 19-year-old girl who worked for him, and he wanted a divorce.

"I was an emotional mess. I never dreamed our ideal marriage could crumble," she explained. "When problems developed, I tried to pray. My two boys needed a daddy, and I needed a husband. But I realized I really didn't know how to pray. I knew all the Bible stories, but I had no grasp of the principles in the Word and certainly no knowledge of the enemy.

"I remember teaching a Bible study on Mary and Martha, and realizing that with all my church work, I was a Martha. I prayed earnestly, 'God, I really want to know You more.' I had no idea what I would go through as He answered that prayer.

"I could do nothing to persuade Jack to change his mind. He wanted a quickie divorce, but I refused. It was two years before the divorce was granted. In the end his drinking and lifestyle led to the loss of his business, and he didn't even marry the girl he'd had the affair with.

"Without the Lord's help I wouldn't have made it. He put a person here and a person there to pray for me and give me helpful books. I learned to pray the Word over my family, and I learned the value of praise. Sitting at the piano, I would play and sing to the Lord, and it was very healing."

After several years Rena met and married Trent, a man with two sons whose wife had abandoned them. Together, they prayed and sought God's help for blending their children into a loving family and learned much about spiritual warfare in the process. It was not an easy road, but God was faithful to see them through, and today Rena and Trent are in full-time ministry together.

"God continues to answer my prayer to know Him more, and He's doing that for all of us," she says with a smile. "All four of our sons are serving the Lord—one works with us in the ministry, three of them are married to godly women, and we have two beautiful grandchildren. He has given us joy and peace in ways I couldn't have dreamed possible."

Claiming the Promised Land

We can compare our experiences in spiritual warfare with those of the children of Israel when God told them to go in and possess Canaan. They found heathen tribes in the Promised Land. God instructed them to drive out the tribes, and He promised to help them win their battles as long as they obeyed Him (see Josh. 23:6-13).

But, sad to say, Israel did not obey God. They compromised with their enemies, intermarried with the Canaanite tribes and took up idol worship and other heathen practices. The tribes they should have driven out became snares for them, and they never fully possessed their Promised Land. In the end they were taken into captivity.

Just as Israel had to fight enemy tribes to possess the land, so Christians today must fight. The difference is, Israel fought flesh-and-blood enemies, while our struggle is against principalities and powers of the unseen world (see Eph. 6:12).

Many Christians hold the notion that once they are believers covered by the blood of Jesus, they are immune to the enemy's influence. True, Jesus' blood cleanses us from all sin. And because we belong to Him, we have authority over all the power of the enemy (see Luke 10:19; Eph. 1:22). But we still have the freedom of choice. At any time, we can choose *not* to obey God and *not* to avail ourselves of the power of the blood of Jesus. That wrong choice makes us vulnerable to the enemy.

Another factor to consider is that we are members of a fallen race. Our basic human weaknesses make us susceptible to the enemy's activity. Though God's great power far exceeds the power of Satan, we humans are no match for the devil if we're operating in our own strength.

More than 300 years ago, Puritan pastor William Gurnall wrote this advice:

> If you are going to take shelter under this attribute [God's almighty power], you must stay within its shade. What good will the shadow of a mighty rock do if we sit in the open sun? That is to say, if we wander away from God's protection by venturing into the heat of temptation, we should not be surprised when our faith grows faint and we stumble and fall into sin. We are weak in ourselves; our strength lies in the rock of God's almightiness. It should be our constant habitation.[7]

It is important to avoid these two extremes: first, blaming the devil for everything that goes wrong, when it could be a result of our own weaknesses or poor choices; second, not recognizing when Satan and his cohorts are at work against us or our loved ones, and failing to take authority over them.

To the degree we choose to walk in our own selfish ways instead of submitting to God's plan and purpose, we allow the enemy to gain a foothold in our lives. Thus Scripture admonishes us, "In your anger do not sin. . . . Do not give the devil a foothold" (Eph. 4:26,27). "Be self-controlled and alert. Your enemy the devil prowls around like a roaring lion looking for someone to devour. Resist him, standing firm in the faith" (1 Pet. 5:8).

Paul shares his experiences of spiritual warfare: "I have fought the good fight, I have finished the race, I have kept the faith. . . . Demas, because he loved this world, has deserted me" (2 Tim. 4:7,10).

Fighting a Battle on Two Fronts

The enemy's attempt to draw us into sin causes our inner conflict. But if we choose to obey God, He gives us success in these skirmishes. Then we are empowered to battle outwardly, dispelling the powers of darkness and setting other captives free. The apostle Paul said he disciplined his body so that sins of his flesh would not cause him to lose that inner battle and be disqualified from doing the Lord's work (see 1 Cor. 9:26-27). We see tragic consequences today in the lives of those who fail to follow Paul's counsel:

- A Bible-school graduate goes back to her old group of friends, and soon she is hooked on drugs again.
- A former missionary leaves his wife and children to become a leader in a New Age group.
- A prominent preacher sternly condemns sin (while winning many converts to the Lord) and then confesses to being addicted to pornography.
- A lawyer with a 20-year record as an excellent Christian businessman is caught embezzling two hundred thousand dollars from the local school board.

Despite these people's exploits for God, they lost the inner contest. They walked out from under the sheltering rock of God's almighty power. Of course the Father's mercy allows for them to be restored and healed. But how much better "to be made new in the attitude of your minds" (Eph. 4:23) and to walk in mastery over these struggles!

God has provided all we need to defeat this adversary of ours—both the enemy within and the enemy without. We have "the full armor of God" (Eph. 6:11) and weapons with "divine power to demolish strongholds" (2 Cor. 10:4).

We women *can* triumph if we choose to employ God's provision and obey His instructions. In the next chapter we will examine the specially designed spiritual wardrobe and weaponry God has prepared for us.

Prayer

Lord, I pray that You will increase my ability to recognize the enemy's attacks and help me to take a stand against his strategies. Protect me from being deceived, and give me greater understanding of how I can stand in the gap on behalf of my loved ones who are under attack. Thank You for being with me continually. Amen.

3

What Our Spiritual Wardrobe Should Look Like

Therefore put on the complete armour of God, so that you may be able to stand your ground on the day of battle, and, having fought to the end, to remain victors on the field. Stand therefore, first fastening round you the girdle of truth and putting on the breastplate of uprightness as well as the shoes of the Good News of peace a firm foundation for your feet. And besides all these take the great shield of faith, on which you will be able to quench all the flaming darts of the Wicked one; and take the helmet of salvation, and the sword of the Spirit which is the word of God. Pray with unceasing prayer and entreaty on every fitting occasion in the Spirit, and be always on the alert to seize opportunities for doing so.

EPHESIANS 6:13-18, *WEYMOUTH*

When we were little girls and played "dress up," we would carefully choose what we put on—from the right shoes to the cutest hat. As grown women, we still like to dress in our best clothes for a special event. But as Christians, we should consider our spiritual wardrobe the most important attire we will ever need to wear. Let's look at *what* it is and *why* we need to be clothed in it daily.

Ephesians 6:13-18 is Paul's warfare handbook—a basic-training manual—for the churches he had founded. He wanted to prepare them for the persecution and adversity he knew would come. Today, this passage is still the best description of the weapons with which we equip ourselves for spiritual conflict.

William Gurnall, a seventeenth-century scholar, wrote:

> It is not left to everyone's fancy to bring whatever weapons he pleases; this would only breed chaos. . . . Look closely at the label to see whether the armor you wear is the workmanship of God or not. There are many imitations on the market nowadays. . . . Do not dare to call anything the armor of God which does not glorify him and defend you against the power of Satan.[1]

The armor Paul speaks of is for our *defense* and protection against evil powers, but God also provides *offensive* weapons. Our warfare wardrobe is complete in every detail. However, it is our responsibility to put it on and to use it.

As mentioned earlier, a surprising number of Christians do not even believe that our spiritual adversary is an actual entity, which of course defies the truth of Scripture (see Luke 4:1-13; Eph. 6:12). Think how dangerous it would be to live in a war zone but refuse to acknowledge the reality of an enemy or his threat to one's survival! Yet that is the state of denial we see many believers in today. It is time for a wake-up call.

The Girdle of Truth

The girdle Paul refers to was actually a wide metal or leather belt worn by a soldier around his lower trunk to hold his armor tightly against his body and to support his sword. It was also used to carry money and other valuables. To "gird up your loins" was to prepare for action (see 1 Sam. 25:13, *KJV*). Truth is the very essence of the gospel: God's plan to free us from sin's bondage through His Son's sacrificial death, burial and resurrection. Jesus said, "Then you will know the truth, and the truth will set you free" (John 8:32).

"If a person's understanding is clear in its hold on truth and his will is sincerely grounded in holy purposes, then he is a maturing Christian," wrote Gurnall. He warned that Satan, as a serpent, assails the truth by sending false teachers who sow error. Or as a lion, he sends persecutors who threaten danger or death in trying to force the believer to deny the truth.[2]

Satan first assaulted the truth in the Garden when he asked Eve, "Did God really say . . . ?" (Gen. 3:1). Not having the belt of truth for armor, she wavered and began to doubt what God had said. Our enemy still uses this subtle weapon of doubt against us. It is "the truth that is in Jesus" (Eph. 4:21) that we must fasten on tightly to protect us from the strategies of the evil one.

Nell's belt of truth slipped when she became fascinated with New Age holistic health and diets. Though she had a Christian upbringing, her pursuit of what she thought was truth soon ensnared her to become involved in a New Age cult.

Her mother, visiting from out of state and discovering the deception, challenged the young man who had lured Nell into the cult group. "My daughter once made a commitment to the Lord Jesus Christ, and she *will* come back to Him and forsake all this garbage you have exposed her to," she told him. "By the power and authority of the blood of Jesus, I bind every influence of Satan you have over my daughter."

When Nell heard about this confrontation, she told her mom, "I want to live my own life, so you and Dad back off my case."

"Honey, we love you too much to let the devil keep you in his clutches," her mom responded. "We'll battle Satan with everything that's in us until the god of this world stops blinding you to the truth, and your will is freed to return to Jesus."

Nell's parents did spiritual warfare every day, commanding Satan to release her. They asked God to place a hedge of protection around her and bring to her remembrance all of the truth she had learned as a young girl. They praised the Lord for being a covenant-keeping God to those who love Him and keep His commandments. They enlisted friends in both states to pray.

One day Nell wandered into a Christian bookstore to buy some health-food cookbooks. "As I was leaving, the store owner insisted I buy a little book, so I did just to get him to leave me alone," she reported. "Later that night I flipped through it and noticed it was full of Scripture verses. The author suggested reading those verses three times a day, like you would take vitamins. I was into anything that would make me healthier, so I did it. Before long those Scripture verses became more important to me than any of the cookbooks or the teachings of the cult."

Five months from the time her parents began spiritual warfare for Nell, she called and asked if she could move back home and start life over again with Jesus. She has since graduated from a Bible school and ministered in several countries, and today she is training her own children in spiritual warfare.

"How easy it was to get deceived when I stopped going to church, praying every day and reading my Bible," she admits. "But, thank God, my eyes were opened to the truth."

The Breastplate of Righteousness

The breastplate is a piece of armor that protected the soldier's heart and other vital organs (today's equivalent would be the bulletproof vest). It was fastened to the girdle, or belt, so it was held securely in place. "Righteousness" simply means "right action," "uprightness" or "conformity to the will of God."[3] It is important to remember that truth and righteousness always go together.

"Watch over your heart with all diligence, for from it flow the springs of life," advised Solomon (Prov. 4:23, *NASB*). Satan often tempts us to compromise our standard of righteousness with such arguments as "But it's for a good cause" or "No one will ever know." The enemy knows that if we compromise the truth and accept his lies, he will gain a foothold in our lives. William Gurnall wrote:

> Righteousness and holiness are God's protection to defend the believer's conscience from all wounds inflicted by sin. . . . Your holiness is what the devil wants to steal from you. . . . He will allow a man to have anything, or be anything, rather than be truly and powerfully holy.[4]

Ruth left her government job because she heard God's call to full-time missions work, but when she arrived on the field, she found that her senior missionary was misusing funds. Ruth had a dilemma: Should she quietly excuse this behavior, or should she stand on principle and risk her friendships, her own credibility and her future in missions? Ruth did the latter for one big reason: She wanted to please God more than she wanted to please people (see Gal. 1:10).

"I was shocked to discover how the devil will work through weak Christians," she said. "It was a very difficult time. Some of my friends thought I was just getting into a power struggle. But I knew that to compromise on this issue to please people would mean displeasing God. Nothing is worth that. I left that organization but continued working in missions, and God met all my needs. The Lord helped me to forgive that woman, and then I 'locked it out with love,' so the enemy couldn't keep bringing the struggle back."

The devil knows the areas where you are vulnerable to compromise in your family relationships, in a job situation, in a friendship or in your church or prayer group. He will make it seem very logical and actually in your own and others' best interests for you to bend your principles a bit.

Speaking to believers, James wrote, "Wash your hands, you sinners, and purify your hearts, you double-minded" (Jas. 4:8b). The compromising hearts of His people—actually a form of spiritual adultery—was and no doubt still is God's greatest grief (see Heb. 3:10). It is a subtle trap indeed. But the soldier who always has his or her breastplate of righteousness firmly in place, secured by the belt of truth, will be protected from a divided heart.

The Gospel Shoes of Peace

Putting on one's shoes is a symbol of readiness. In Paul's day, shoes weren't worn indoors (and still aren't in many Eastern cultures). To put on your shoes indicated you were going outside the protection of the house. God told His people to eat the Passover with their shoes on, so they would be ready to flee Egypt (see Exod. 12:11). The soldier's shoes protected his feet and usually were fitted with metal cleats to make him more sure-footed in combat.

One commentator notes that the word translated "shod" in the *New King James Version* of Ephesians 6:15 comes from a compound Greek word meaning "binding something very tightly on the bottom of one's feet."[5] He continues with this observation:

> Paul uses this illustration to tell us that we must firmly tie *God's peace* onto our lives. If we only give peace a loosely fitting position in our lives, it won't be long before the affairs of life knock our peace out of place. Hence, we must bind peace onto our minds and emotions in the same way Roman soldiers made sure to *bind* their shoes very tightly onto their feet. . . . [Thus] you will be empowered to keep marching ahead, oblivious to the devil's attempts to take you down![6]

This important piece of the Christian's armor is crucial when navigating through the war zone of life. Joyce's shoes of peace enabled her to walk serenely through the "mine field" of her husband's wrath. During a visit to her parents' home, Joyce and Barry were alone in the house one day when he went to take a shower.

Because Joyce was running the washing machine, Barry got a burst of cold water that threw him into an unreasonable rage. Forgetting that the bathroom door was ajar and that Joyce was within earshot, he began screaming curses at her and calling her names. It was a gush of profanity that seemed demonic.

Joyce immediately began calling on God, asking, "Lord, how do I handle this?" She went to the living room and began running the vacuum cleaner while she prayed and bound the spirits of hatred and rage.

"I felt the Lord tell me, 'Walk in the opposite spirit,'" she said. "Barry was operating in a spirit of hate and condemnation; I needed to operate in a spirit of love and forgiveness. I forgave Barry for the cutting things he had said. By the time he came out of the bathroom, I truly had received God's peace."

As Barry was leaving to go wash his car, Joyce offered to go along and help. "I cleaned all the windows on his car, inside and out, and he had no clue that he had upset me. When we got back to the house, I confronted him with what I had heard. I was able to stand my ground and do it calmly. He didn't apologize or express any regret whatsoever. He just glared at me and said, 'I didn't know you heard,' and walked away. That experience showed me just how hardened his heart had become, but it also showed me that God's peace can sustain me no matter what happens."

We have the assurance of Scripture that "the peace of God, which transcends all understanding, will guard [our] hearts and [our] minds in Christ Jesus" (Phil. 4:7).

The Shield of Faith

Various kinds of shields were in use in Paul's day, but the specific one Paul refers to in Ephesians 6 is the large rectangular shield that could protect the entire body. It was common practice for the soldier to anoint his shield with oil, so it would reflect the sun's rays and blind the enemy, and this would also help deflect the enemy's blows. Gurnall gave this insight concerning the shield:

> The apostle compares faith to a shield because . . . the shield is intended for the defense of the whole body. . . . And if the shield was not large enough to cover every part at once, the skillful soldier could turn it this way or that way, to stop the swords or the arrows, no matter where they were directed. . . . Not only does the shield defend the whole body, but it defends the soldier's other armor also. . . . Every grace derives its safety from faith; each one lies secure under the shadow of faith.[7]

It is important that we have faith in God—not faith in faith. Our confidence in God must be based on His character and trustworthiness, not on our own ability to follow a formula. Scripture tells us, "Without faith it is impossible to please God, because anyone who comes to him must believe that he exists and that he rewards those who earnestly seek him" (Heb. 11:6).

Because she grew up in a dysfunctional family and suffered abuse as a child, Chris was tormented with thoughts of suicide, even after she became a Christian. Through prayer and counseling, the oppression lifted, and she was free.

"Then I learned that the enemy always tests your deliverance," she said. "Though I knew the Holy Spirit had powerfully ministered to me, I would occasionally have thoughts of suicide again. I had to use the shield of faith to deflect those fiery darts. Over and over I would say to the enemy, 'Satan, I resist you. I *have* been delivered in Jesus' name. I will live and not die. You are defeated, and I command you to flee.' I persisted until the enemy finally stopped bothering me in that area. I am totally free."

The foundation of our faith is in Scripture: "Faith comes by hearing, and hearing by the word of God" (Rom. 10:17, *NKJV*). So the more thoroughly we are immersed in God's Word, the stronger our faith will be. Simply put, faith means believing that God is who He says He is and that He will do what He says He will do!

The Helmet of Salvation

The helmet not only protected the soldier's head in battle but also bore insignia or symbols identifying which army he belonged to. Paul instructed, "Let us be self-controlled, putting on . . . the hope of salvation as a helmet" (1 Thess. 5:8). This hope, or helmet, of salvation protects the Christian against attacks on the mind, one of Satan's primary targets.

To deal with such an attack we must learn to distinguish the voice of our enemy from God's voice. God will speak words of love, comfort, conviction and guidance. The enemy speaks words of fear, accusation and condemnation. Gwen's story is an example of how to repel Satan's attack on the mind.

Gwen, her husband and their 13-year-old grandson, Mark (whom they had adopted), were in their van heading home after a holiday visit to relatives. What had been a wonderful visit had gone sour just as they were saying their good-byes. Mark had been playing outdoors with his young cousins, one of whom got slightly hurt in a moment of Mark's carelessness. The child's mother gave Mark a tongue-lashing and embarrassed him in front of everyone.

The three of them got into the van with sagging spirits to begin their eight-hundred-mile journey in miserable silence. Mark slumped on the seat as far back in the van as he could get. As they rode along, Gwen glanced out her window and saw a reflection of herself in the glass. In her mind she heard a voice say, "You're old and fat and ugly." Studying the image for a moment she thought to herself, *It's true, Gwen. You are old and fat and ugly.*

But suddenly she had a flash of insight. *That's a spirit of rejection! It came in with Mark, and it will stay with us all the way home if I permit it to,* she thought.

"I immediately bound the spirit of rejection and commanded it to flee, and then I prayed quietly," she reported. "In a very short time the whole atmosphere inside the van changed. Mark clambered up to the front seat and began laughing and talking with us, and we enjoyed the trip home together. Had I not resisted that attack against my mind, I would have played right into the enemy's hand."

Dean Sherman's analogy is helpful:

Every military post has guards. They stand quietly at their posts until they hear a rustling in the bushes. Then they immediately ask: "Who goes there?" and are prepared to evict any intruder. We too need to post a guard at the gate of our minds to check the credentials of every thought and every imagination, ready to cast down that which is not true, not righteous, or not of God. If it doesn't belong, out it goes. This is spiritual warfare: being alert to every thought.[8]

The Sword of the Spirit

The sword is used not only to defend against the enemy but also to offensively attack him. Paul's sword is the Word of God—the *rhema*. W. E. Vine says:

The significance of *rhema* (as distinct from *logos*) is exemplified in the injunction to take "the sword of the Spirit, which is the word of God" (Eph. 6:17); here the reference is not to the whole Bible as such, but to the individual Scripture which the Spirit brings to our remembrance for use in time of need, a prerequisite being the regular storing of the mind with Scripture.[9]

Lynn used the sword of the Spirit to resist a physical assault. As she was getting ready for bed one night while her husband, Jay, took the babysitter home, she felt an urge to pray, not knowing why. "Lord, what is this I'm feeling?" she asked. "Show me how to pray."

"Pray against a spirit of harassment," responded that still, small voice. She prayed accordingly, and after feeling a sense of release, she got into bed. Within a few minutes, she heard people coming up the stairs. *Who is Jay bringing home with him at this hour?* she wondered.

The next thing she knew, a strange man knelt beside her bed and held a pistol pressed to her neck. His companion, holding Jay at gunpoint, ripped out the phone cord. "Just do as he says, Lynn," Jay said quietly, "and everything will be all right."

"Give me your rings," commanded the thief as he began trying to pull them off Lynn's finger.

Forgetting Jay's advice, Lynn answered, "No! In Jesus' name, you can't have my wedding rings!"

"Then his hands drew near to touch my body," she said. "Thoughts of rape, blood and even death entered my mind. As quickly as those thoughts came, Scriptures flowed into my heart. Although I was shaking, the promises of God filled my spirit, and total peace flooded my being. Repeatedly the man drew near, and it was as if an invisible force prevented him from going any further.

"I lay crying softly in bed, with the gun still pointed to my throat, marveling that my two small children and baby were sleeping soundly and that my emotions hadn't carried me into a screaming, terrified frenzy. The other burglar went through the house, gathering whatever he thought had any value. After what seemed forever, the man backed away from my bedside, left the room and closed the door."

After waiting for some time, Lynn and Jay crept out to survey what was left of their plundered home. To their surprise, they found all their belongings piled on the living-room floor. Only a few pieces of jewelry were missing. Lynn and Jay wondered whether God had sent some noise, or perhaps an angel, to scare the thieves away. To this day, the mystery remains.

"Jay had established the habit of praying aloud every time we left our house or car, 'Lord, please station Your angels to guard and protect our belongings,'" Lynn concluded. "God proved to us once again that He alone is our security."

Wielding the Sword

Josette had an opportunity to use the sword of the Spirit as an offensive weapon when her son, Troy, began having difficulty with his boss on his new job and called home for prayer. Using verses from Daniel, Josette began to pray, "Father, may Troy find favor and compassion with his boss. May he be well informed, quick to understand and qualified for the job. May he be found 10 times better than others" (see Dan. 1:4,9,20).

Her prayer continued, "Satan, I block your tactics with the Word of God. My son is a mighty man of valor! God promises him prosperity. I bind the spirits of pride and jealousy in his boss that are coming against Troy. You will not hinder God's plan for him. Thank You, Lord, that Troy will be Your representative on this job and that he is becoming the man of God You created him to be."

Josette continued praying in this way as the Lord gave her additional Scriptures, and Troy's situation gradually improved. Fourteen months later, when Troy was promoted to a job in another city, his boss gave him a farewell party and bragged about how qualified and well-informed Troy was in his work—a specific answer to his mother's prayers!

As many people's experiences attest, the Word of God is not only a spiritual weapon but also a source of great comfort. Arthur Mathews presents this challenge:

> If we accept the fact that our role in life is that of soldiers, then we must drop our toys and become more acquainted with the weapons of our warfare. In a conflict situation a soldier's best friend is his weapon, because it is his one resource for disposing of the enemy, securing his own safety, and accomplishing the will of his captain.[10]

He then quotes missionary Amy Carmichael:

> The only thing that matters is to throw all the energies of our being into the faithful use of this precious blade. Then, and only then, may we "rest our cause upon His Holy Word."[11]

For as long as we are on this earth, we will need to wear our armor and wield our sword. As William Gurnall wrote so concisely, "Once [the Christian] enters the gates of that glorious city, he can say, 'Armor was for earth but robes are for heaven.'"[12]

Prayer

Lord, I am so grateful for the armor You provide to protect us from the enemy. Help me to gain a deeper understanding of the power of the Word, our principal weapon, as I build up an arsenal of Scriptures to use in warfare. Because I know You are with me, I declare the enemy's plans will come to nothing. Amen.

How Strong Can
a Woman Be?

*The Lord gives the word [of power]; the women who bear
and publish [the news] are a great host.*

PSALM 68:11, *AMP*

Ten thousand people were asked in a poll, "Who has had the most positive influence on your religious faith?" "My mother" was the most frequent answer from every age group. "My wife" was the second-place response from men. The survey also revealed that women have a higher faith level than men.[1] This poll simply proves what most of us knew all along: Women have a great deal of influence for God—which is both a privilege and a responsibility!

In Psalm 68:11, the word "women" is sometimes rendered "company," which is a military word. But this is not a conventional company of women soldiers. A loose translation of the verse would be, "The women who proclaim the news of victory are an army of praisers." Women may be considered less muscular than men, but our praising, praying and proclaiming of the good news have the power to push back the forces that seek to destroy our loved ones and our communities!

Why is it that we are so influential? Our theory is that because women were created to give birth in the natural realm, we know more about travailing and giving birth in the spiritual realm. We tend to feel things deeply, are readily moved with compassion and have a high tolerance for pain. Women warriors have the tenacity to stick it out until the birthing is done and loved ones are brought from darkness into the light of Jesus.

"The hand that rocks the cradle is the hand that rules the world," wrote poet William Ross Wallace. We could paraphrase his thought: The one who "gives birth" in the spiritual realm is the one who prevails over the powers of darkness!

Hurling Stones at the Enemy

We've all heard stories of a woman performing a feat of superhuman strength, such as lifting the back of a car when her child was in danger. The maternal instinct sends a surge of adrenaline through a woman, empowering her to do something thought impossible even for a well-muscled man. How much greater is the power the Holy Spirit gives to enable us in spiritual warfare!

Edith, a petite, graying mother, was puttering around her kitchen around 9:30 one Friday morning when a cold chill swept over her. Fear gripped her heart. "Dale is in danger," a voice said inside her. She immediately began praying for her engineer son. Five . . . ten . . . fifteen minutes she prayed. Then the burden lifted, and she went back to washing dishes.

That evening, Dale called to tell her about his day. Around 9:30 that morning, while inspecting some remodeling work in the manufacturing plant where he worked, he suddenly felt an urge to move out of the way. As he stepped aside, a huge steel beam fell to the floor, striking the very spot where he had been standing seconds before.

In the natural realm, Dale's little mom never could have deflected the fall of that steel beam. But because Edith was sensitive to the voice of the Holy Spirit as she worked in her kitchen that morning, her son's life was spared.

Edith's story brings to mind the Old Testament account of the Israelite woman who, when she saw King Abimelech approaching her city to burn it, took immediate action. Watching him from the top of the Tower of Thebez, she picked up an upper millstone and hurled it down on the wicked king's head. Too proud to have it said that a woman killed him, the king ordered his armor bearer to draw his sword and finish him off (see Judg. 9:50-54; 2 Sam. 11:21).

Never let it be said that women are weak! They are still hurling stones at the enemy's plans. This unnamed woman of Thebez is one of a large company of women who continue to wreak havoc with Satan's plans.

Standing Against the Enemy's Flood

I (Ruthanne) learned years ago during a crisis how strong a woman can be, though I didn't feel strong at the time. For months I had been studying about spiritual warfare and learning about our authority in Christ. But I was yet to put this truth to the test.

One October day when heavy rains hit our area, local radio stations warned of flash flooding. That afternoon it was time for me to drive the car pool to pick up kids from school, but my husband volunteered to go instead because of the bad weather. Just after he left, the rain began to fall even harder, thundering like Niagara Falls. Looking out the front door, I saw that water had filled the street and was now pouring over the curb, down our sloping yard toward the house. Muddy water flooded our sidewalk and was quickly rising to porch level.

In a panic, I tried to brace a board across the porch entrance and then laid towels over the threshold of the front door. In seconds, the rising water swept the board away and crept onto our small porch.

Suddenly I felt a righteous anger in my spirit and realized I needed to take authority over the enemy's attempt to damage our home. With no time to call my prayer partner or look up a Scripture verse, I just had to wing it.

"Devil, in the name of Jesus, I forbid you to enter this house with muddy flood water," I shouted into the storm as I stood at the open front door. "This house belongs to God. It has been dedicated to Him, and you have no right to enter and destroy it. In Jesus' name, I command this water to recede."

When I stopped shouting, I realized the thundering noise had diminished and the rain was slackening. The water had come up to the threshold, and the towels were wet. But as I watched, the flood-water receded from the porch, formed a whirlpool below the step, and then ran down the walkway, around the corner of the house and down the driveway.

For a moment I stood rooted to the spot, almost in shock that my desperate tactic had worked. Then I began to praise God for His faithfulness, acknowledging that He had given the victory. My husband and son were amazed when they got home and saw the mud silt on the porch that confirmed my story.

The following year we had another season of heavy rain with flash-flood warnings. I began taking authority over the devil as soon as I heard the news, declaring our home off-limits to his destructive work. Though more rain fell that week than we'd had the previous October, floodwaters never threatened our house. I learned the effectiveness of engaging in spiritual warfare before a situation reaches crisis proportions.

Of course, we have no power on our own; we must rely on the Holy Spirit's power. But operating in faith, not fear, is one way to overcome the enemy's harassment. I might add that I don't believe we are to indiscriminately "take authority " over the weather. (In fact, in this case I didn't command the rain to cease.) But this kind of action is appropriate in situations when we're led by the Holy Spirit.

Now that I live in a different part of Texas, one where drought is a common problem, we often pray for rain. But when bad storms threaten, I ask the Lord to send the needed rain without any destruction to life or property.

Can God Use Me?

What can one woman do? We've already looked at Deborah and the difference she made in the nation of Israel. Scripture gives many more accounts of women who wielded godly influence in significant ways: Jochebed, Miriam, Hannah, Huldah, Esther, Ruth, Elizabeth, Mary, Dorcas, Priscilla, Phoebe and Joanna, among others.

It should also be noted that the godly influence of these women wasn't always just through prayer. Sometimes prayer and action were needed! This holds true for today.

Helen, an Alabama farmer's wife, is one such woman. Her commitment to prayer—and action—has literally changed people's lives. Bonnie was one of them. With a hard-working husband, two lovely children, a home and many church friends, Bonnie seemed to have everything required for happiness. But because of childhood molestation by her father, she had allowed the seeds of hatred to grow in her heart until that hatred extended to include all men. Turning to other women for love and acceptance, she'd gotten involved in lesbianism.

Bonnie became a Christian and got married, but she still struggled with affections for her former lovers. She even preferred to dress like a male, but her ambivalent feelings made her so miserable that she came to Helen for help.

No matter how many Scriptures Helen showed her to the contrary, however, Bonnie refused to admit that lesbianism is a sin. One day after five hours of prayer and ministry to no avail, Helen told her, "I'm going to pray a prayer as though I'm you, and I want you to repeat it after me: Dear heavenly Father, I see in Your Word that homosexuality is a sin. Therefore, lesbianism is a sin. Please forgive me for committing this sin."

"I can't say that because I don't think it is so," Bonnie argued, shaking her head.

Finally, after persistent prayer, Bonnie got the words out of her mouth: "It is a sin. It is a sin. God, please forgive me." At last she began to sob as the healing power of Jesus' forgiveness engulfed her. Soon afterward, Helen took her to a women's conference, where Bonnie experienced godly love and affection from women, and a new life of freedom began for her.

Helen remained a strong force of love in Bonnie's life, showing her that she could have a healthy relationship with a woman friend. She helped her redecorate her home; then they worked on Bonnie's appearance—hairstyle, makeup and clothes. Helen and her husband helped her plant a garden and later can some of the vegetables she grew. When Bonnie's husband returned from a tour of duty overseas, he hardly recognized his wife, but he rejoiced at the changes.

Now, after completing graduate school, Bonnie helps other people through her counseling ministry. Helen's willingness to stick it out with this tough case—her perseverance in prayer and action—is a powerful example of what one woman with Jesus can do.

Enlarging Our Borders

Perhaps you feel your circle of influence is pretty small—consisting of your husband, your children, their school, your extended family, your church, your friends. If you are single, your sphere may consist primarily of your work relationships, your family, your friends and your church. If you're an empty nester or a widow, you may feel your world is shrinking.

Have you ever considered that God might want to expand your horizon? To use you to pray not only for your family and friends but also for your city, state, nation or another nation of the world?

I (Quin) remember how God began enlarging my borders some years ago. My husband's job had taken us to a different town, which I really didn't like very well. I complained to the Lord about it one day.

Later, in my morning Bible reading, I stumbled across Jeremiah's message to God's people living in exile. It jumped from the page into my heart: "Build houses and settle down . . . seek the peace and prosperity of the city to which I have carried you into exile. Pray to the LORD for it, because if it prospers, you too will prosper" (Jer. 29:5-7).

Pray for the city where God had brought me? How could I? Where would I start? Because I knew nothing about spiritual warfare in those days, I just began praying about things I read in the daily newspaper. Not a bad place to start, really.

A year later we moved to another area. In my Bible reading one day, verses from Isaiah sprang to life and challenged me to begin praying very specifically for the city where I now lived: "I have set watchmen upon your walls, O Jerusalem, who will never hold their peace day or night; you who [are His servants and by your prayers] put the Lord in remembrance [of His promises], keep not silence, and give Him no rest until He establishes Jerusalem and makes her a praise in the earth" (Isa. 62:6-7, *AMP*).

In place of "Jerusalem," I put the name of my city. And I wrote in my Bible: "God wants to station me as an intercessor sentry—a guard to watch in prayer for my family and city. I'll need God's strategy to ambush the enemy's plan."

Taking Stock of the City

I did some research on our sprawling resort area, and then one day after fasting and prayer, a friend and I took a prayer walk in a two-block area of downtown. We passed an antique store with statues of Buddha in the window, a liquor store with a sign that read "In Booze We Trust," a New Age store with a window display of crystals and weird head sculptures, a secret lodge temple, a Native American museum and burial mound, and an amusement palace with huge carved tikis. Of course, not everything associated with Native American and other ethnic groups is demonic, but the enemy has infiltrated most cultures of the world. My heart was broken to see in only a two-block area so many things that surely were not honoring to God. Yet I realized that not too many years ago, when I was in the enemy's camp, I would have thought all this was fine.

As we walked, we bound the enemy's works of darkness and deception and asked the Holy Spirit to bring a revelation of Jesus Christ to the hearts of the people. Later we walked up and down and prayed on nearby streets, where psychics, go-go dancers, nightclubs and liquor stores catered to summer tourists.

In time we enlisted other women who shared our vision to see righteousness become the standard for the city. Walking in pairs, we covered malls, schools, government buildings, residential neighborhoods, beaches and parks.

Over the next few months a fortune-teller went out of business, one psychic shop shut down, and a teen nightclub closed its doors. We heard of other results later on, but of course we won't know the full effect of our spiritual warfare until we get to heaven. Though I have since moved, my prayer partners continue standing against darkness in that city, and others are catching the vision that they can make a difference through prayer.

John Dawson, author of *Taking Our Cities for God*, writes:

The fact is, there is a battle raging over your city and it is affecting you right now. Our individual blind spots and vices are usually common to the culture around us, and that culture is influenced by what the Bible calls principalities and powers (Eph. 6:12, *KJV*). . . . Spiritual warfare begins at a personal level and escalates through layers of increasing difficulty—from personal and family to the realm of church life, and beyond that to the collective church in the city and the national and international realms.

Have you ever thought about the battle for your immediate neighborhood? . . . Several years ago my staff and I went on a prayer walk around our neighborhood. We stood in front of every house, rebuked Satan's work in Jesus' name, and prayed for a revelation of Jesus in the life of each family. We are still praying. . . . Today there are at least nine Christian families in the block where I live, and there is a definite sense of the Lord's peace.[2]

Repentance and Corporate Prayer

Nehemiah gives us an example of one person confessing the sins of his nation. When he learned that the enemy still had access to Jerusalem, some 800 miles away from where he was living in exile, he wept, mourned, fasted and prayed because of the condition of his homeland. He even confessed the sins of his forefathers (see Neh. 1:6-7). Then he took action, getting permission and funding to go rally his people still living in Jerusalem to help rebuild the broken-down wall. They accomplished the task in record time, despite their enemies' opposition.

God will give you a prayer from His heart to pray in repentance for our nation. Here's how one woman prayed: "God, we are truly sorry for the way our nation has gone against Your biblical principles. Forgive us for the sins of abortion, same-sex marriages, lawlessness, bribery and discrimination and for passing laws that are contrary to Your commandments. Have mercy on us, forgive our sins, and help us restore our nation to one of righteousness."

Once on a prayer journey to Washington, I (Quin) joined more than four thousand Christian women for a two-hour prayer gathering on the steps of the United States Capitol building. First we prayed for our nation. We asked God to give wisdom, knowledge and understanding to all our government leaders. We engaged in warfare against principalities and powers of darkness that have allowed abortion on demand, racism, humanism in our schools, widespread drug abuse and an increase in crime, pornography, child abuse and missing children.

Then we prayed for the women of America—the married, the divorced, the widowed, the single. We prayed for working mothers, for abused wives, for the wives and women of the military. We asked God to minister to their deepest needs and reveal Himself to them.

We did not demonstrate or hold up signs; we just prayed. Afterward, small groups of women walked around the Capitol grounds, praying for those who work there, and then small groups of women did the same around the White House, the Supreme Court and various embassies. We prayed quietly for God's purposes to be accomplished in our nation.

It is meaningful to walk the ground where the devil is operating as we assault him and make an outward declaration of God's victory in that place. As Joshua was about to march into the Promised Land, God told him: "I will give you every place where you set your foot, as I promised Moses. . . . Be strong and courageous, because you will lead these people to inherit the land. . . . Do not be terrified; do not be discouraged, for the LORD your God will be with you wherever you go" (Josh. 1:3,6,9).

We can act upon this word today as the Holy Spirit shows us where to set our foot and enables us to keep an attitude of humility and repentance as we pursue such a prayer project.

Battle in the Heavenlies

A big obstacle for many women in maintaining a consistent prayer life is the nagging question, "How can *my* prayers possibly make a difference in the way things turn out?" It is one of Satan's biggest ploys to dissuade us from pursuing prayer. Yet Scripture clearly shows us that when believers pray on earth, they instigate activity in the heavenlies.

Daniel 10 describes the time the prophet Daniel had an angelic visitation after three weeks of praying, fasting and repenting on behalf of his people. The angel told Daniel that on the first day he humbled himself to pray, God had heard his words. In fact, the angel had been dispatched with a response to Daniel's prayer, but he had encountered interference from "the prince of the Persian kingdom" (Dan. 10:13). The messenger angel had to have help from the angel Michael to get through. He delivered a prophetic message to Daniel and indicated that on his return, he would fight both the prince of Persia and the prince of Greece (see Dan. 10:20).

If there were rulers in the spiritual realm (called princes) trying to stop Daniel's prayers from being answered, are we immune? No! Hostile spiritual forces—the principalities and powers Paul speaks of in Ephesians 6:12—still try to block our prayers from being answered. And Scripture implies that these evil princes rule over different geographical areas.

When you go on a prayer walk, ask the Holy Spirit to reveal to you the spirits needing to be bound in that area. Then ask God to open blinded eyes so that people might turn from darkness to light and receive forgiveness through Jesus.

The Comforter Has Come

The gift of the Holy Spirit empowers us to be strong women of God, even in our moments of weakness. Jesus promised His followers, "I will ask the Father, and He will give you another Comforter (Counselor, Helper, Intercessor, Advocate, Strengthener, and Standby), that He may remain with you forever—the Spirit of Truth. . . . He will teach you all things" (John 14:16-17,26, *AMP*).

Without this gift of the Holy Spirit, we would be powerless before the enemy. But He strengthens us for battle in many ways. Here are a few of them:

- The Holy Spirit testifies of Jesus (John 15:26; Rom. 8:16).
- The Holy Spirit teaches (Luke 12:12; 1 Cor. 2:13).

- The Holy Spirit guides (Matt. 10:19-20; John 16:13).
- The Holy Spirit reveals (John 14:20; 1 Cor. 2:9-10).
- The Holy Spirit comforts (John 14:26; Acts 9:31).
- The Holy Spirit gives joy (John 15:11; Rom. 14:17).
- The Holy Spirit gives spiritual gifts (1 Cor. 12:4-31).
- The Holy Spirit liberates (John 8:32; Rom. 8:2).
- The Holy Spirit empowers for service (Luke 4:14; Acts 1:8).
- The Holy Spirit intercedes for us (Rom. 8:26; 1 Cor. 14:14-15).

Many believe that when we ask the Holy Spirit to intercede through us, we are to seek God's will and then pray accordingly. Still others believe it involves praying in an unknown tongue as those in the early Christian church did. Of course both ideas are valid, and it is important to discuss this particular "weapon."

Consider Paul's words: "The Spirit helps us in our weakness. We do not know what we ought to pray for, but the Spirit himself intercedes for us with groans that words cannot express. And he who searches our hearts knows the mind of the Spirit, because the Spirit intercedes for the saints in accordance with God's will" (Rom. 8:26b, 27). "I will pray with the spirit, and I will pray with the understanding also" (1 Cor. 14:15a, *KJV*).

Interceding according to the will of God is the most important ingredient of prayer and the key to effectiveness. Pastor Judson Cornwall explains the use of tongues in prayer:

Prayer is the most valuable use of tongues for it is "speaking to God" (1 Cor. 14:2). . . . The Holy Spirit is certainly not limited to the English language, nor is He confined to modern languages. He has access to every language ever used by mankind, and He is very familiar with the language used in heaven. When deep intercession is needed, the Spirit often uses a language that is beyond the intellectual grasp of the speaker to bypass the censorship of his or her conscious mind, thereby enabling the Spirit to say what needs to be prayed without arguing with the faith level of the one through whom the intercession flows.

Praying in tongues is not the work of the subconscious. It's really *supra-intellectual* praying. That is, the prayer is beyond the natural mind, not beneath the conscious level. Intercessory prayer in tongues is not incoherent speech. The very words are motivated by the Holy Spirit, addressed to the Father and approved by the Lord Jesus (see Mark 16:17).[3]

According to Acts 2:39 the gift is available to all born-again Christians—not just those who lived in the first century after Christ. The only requirements are that you be God's child and that you ask (see Luke 11:11-13). We should use the gift of praying in the Spirit, not just during regular devotional times, but whenever we sense a need for prayer as we go about our daily activities.

Strategy for Warfare

By now you've gotten the idea that every battle differs, as does the strategy for each battle. The Lord loves a tenacious warrior who is ready to take on an assignment at a moment's notice and who will seek His direction for strategy and timing. One friend suggests three principles to help us keep our warfare in proper perspective:

1. **A**ggression toward the enemy
2. **R**uthlessness with our own fleshly pride and selfishness
3. **T**olerance and love toward one another

Thus we have an acrostic, the ART of spiritual warfare. How strong can a woman be? As strong as she will allow the Holy Spirit to be through her. But becoming that vessel the Holy Spirit can use requires discipline. And that's the topic of our next chapter.

Prayer

Thank You, Lord, for providing the power of the Holy Spirit to enable me to fulfill my prayer assignments. Please give me clear strategy and timing for every battle I face. Help me always to walk in humility and depend on Your strength and wisdom, not my own. I praise You, Lord—the captain of our salvation— for Your promise of victory. Amen.

The Disciplines of the Spirit-Empowered Woman

"For if you remain silent at this time, relief and deliverance for the Jews will arise from another place, but you and your father's family will perish. And who knows but that you have come to royal position for such a time as this?" Then Esther sent this reply to Mordecai ... "I and my maids will fast as you do. When this is done, I will go to the king. ... And if I perish, I perish."

ESTHER 4:14-16

Queen Esther is a biblical example of how strong a woman can be. When facing a crisis that threatened the annihilation of the Jews, she called for a period of fasting and prayer before she took any action on her own. Then she put her life on the line by going to the king and intervening for her people's lives.

Perhaps the greatest lessons we can learn from Esther are *discipline* and *balance*. She did not rush to implement a plan of her own without seeking God's direction. Nor did she take a passive role and say, "If God wants to do something, He can do it." Disciplining herself and her people through a fast, she balanced that by taking action one step at a time.

Discipline and Destiny

Esther's story provides an excellent model for fighting our own tough spiritual battles. Long before she was selected as one of the candidates to be queen, Esther had learned the discipline of obedience. She willingly obeyed instructions from Mordecai, her foster father. Then she submitted to a disciplined year of preparation before she was presented to the king. Even after being crowned queen of Persia, she continued to follow Mordecai's godly counsel.

When Mordecai conveyed to her Haman's edict calling for all the Jews to be killed on a certain day, he asked her to go before the king and plead for mercy. Esther was reluctant to do so, because such boldness could jeopardize her life, but Mordecai's appeal that perhaps she was now in the palace for this very purpose caused her to take the challenge. Shortly thereafter, she called for God's people to join her in three days of fasting. As the story unfolds, we see that Esther was following three important principles:

1. She settled in her heart that this battle was one in which she should be involved. She was in the palace "for such a time as this," and her commitment was solid.

2. She called the Jewish people to a fast, recognizing a solution was beyond her human wisdom. She would have to rely totally upon God.

3. She took action one step at a time, trusting God for His direction at each juncture.

God granted Esther favor when she went to the king unbidden, and he held out his scepter to receive her. But instead of immediately presenting her petition, she invited the king and Haman to a banquet she had prepared. At the table that evening, she still didn't reveal her request, though the king gave her the opportunity. Obviously she was aware of the importance of timing. She simply asked the two men to come to another banquet the following day.

Then God intervened by giving the king a sleepless night and causing him to learn of a long-forgotten favor Mordecai had done for him. It was a case of God revealing at a critical moment something that had long been hidden. Totally unaware of God's strategy, Esther simply had to keep her trust in Him. The ensuing events caused the tables to be turned on wicked Haman, and he ended by being hung on the very gallows he had built for Mordecai, who was now honored as a hero (see Esther 6–9).

This was a victory far greater than Esther could have imagined. She did the possible, while God did the seemingly impossible to "reverse the curse" against the Jews, and they were spared.

In the end, Haman's entire estate was given to Esther, and Mordecai was promoted to second in command under the king.

Why Fast Anyway?

As we mentioned, Esther's immediate response to crisis was to call for a three-day fast in preparation for her going before the king. It seems quite plausible that during those three days, God revealed to her the strategy she was to follow. In like manner, fasting can become a weapon of warfare for us to receive God's guidance and strategy for our intercession and spiritual battles.

The prophetess Anna is an example of an intercessor who, like Esther, was in the right place at the right time. For years she had been in the Temple, ministering to the Lord with fasting and prayers.

One day, the Spirit led Anna to enter a certain area of the Temple at the exact moment Mary and Joseph arrived with the infant Jesus. Recognizing that He was indeed the promised Messiah, Anna was the first woman to broadcast the good news (see Luke 2:36-38). Her years of prayer and fasting were richly rewarded.

However, fasting is not limited to just being a way to wage spiritual warfare or a way to minister to the Lord. *Dake's Annotated Reference Bible* offers the view that fasting is also the antidote for unbelief:

> The disciples asked the Lord why they could not heal a lunatic boy. Jesus said, "Because of your unbelief. . . . Howbeit this kind goeth not out but by prayer and fasting" (Matt. 17:20-21, *KJV*). Faith needs prayer for its development and full growth, and prayer needs fasting for the same reason. This is a biblical doctrine. To fast means to abstain from food—that which caused the fall of man.
>
> Fasting humbles the soul before God, chastens the soul, and crucifies the appetites and denies them so as to give time to prayer. It manifests earnestness before God to the exclusion of all else, shows obedience, gives the digestive system a rest, demonstrates the mastery of man over appetites, aids in temptation, helps to attain power over demons, develops faith, crucifies unbelief, and aids in prayer.[1]

Some Christians are reluctant to fast because they fear it can lead to fanaticism or occultism. We are aware that fasting is practiced by spiritists and adherents of false religions to sharpen their sensitivities to the spiritual realm and even to invite demons to give them power. But Jesus spoke of fasting at the same time He taught His followers how to pray and how to give. All three are disciplines the Christian should observe (see Matt. 6:1-18).

In his excellent book *God's Chosen Fast*, Arthur Wallis writes:

> We must not think of fasting as a hunger strike designed to force God's hand and get our own way! Prayer, however, is more complex than simply asking a loving father to supply his child's needs. Prayer is warfare. Prayer is wrestling. There are opposing forces. There are spiritual cross currents. . . .

The man who prays with fasting is giving heaven notice that he is truly in earnest; that he will not give up nor let God go without the blessing. . . .

You should expect that a season of fasting would prove to be for you, as it was for your Master, a time of conflict with the powers of darkness. Satan will often try to take advantage of your physical condition to launch an attack. Discouragement is one of his weapons. Guard against it by maintaining a spirit of praise.[2]

We see that setting captives free also is a scriptural purpose for fasting. God asks, "Is not this the kind of fasting I have chosen: to loose the chains of injustice and untie the cords of the yoke, to set the oppressed free and break every yoke?" (Isa. 58:6).

Pushing Back the Enemy

Erby, a modern-day Anna, experienced the power of fasting and prayer in the lives of Pastor Sam Phillips and his wife, Gloria, who suffered from a crippling disease and subsequent discouragement.

Soon after Erby started working for the Phillips family as a housekeeper, she began praying daily that they would receive the enabling power of the Holy Spirit in their lives. But the Lord expressly warned Erby not to open her mouth to Sam and Gloria about spiritual matters. Also, she was not to open her mouth to eat anything on the days she worked for them. She was to pray—period.

Many days Erby fussed with God for making her fast and keep quiet about spiritual things when she saw so many opportunities to speak. But He would not grant her that liberty. For four years Erby never opened her mouth to Sam and Gloria; but oh, how she talked to God! Meanwhile, Gloria seemed to be getting worse.

Erby would clean the household furniture, praying as she went, claiming that its owners would make a deeper commitment to Jesus. She prayed over their bathtub, their drapes, their doorknobs, their refrigerator and their sink. To Erby, the Phillips's whole house became an altar of prayer. She sanctified every inch of it and kept commanding the devil to move back and take his hands off God's property.

The day came when Gloria spoke sharply to Erby and then hobbled off to her bedroom to end her misery with a handful of pills. The Lord showed Erby what was about to happen, but still He made her keep quiet. She cried out, "Oh, God! By Your Holy Spirit, I know what's about to happen in that room! I can't go in there, but You can, Lord. I ask You in the power of the name of Jesus to go in and stop what is about to take place."

God heard Erby's supplications. Gloria did not swallow the fistful of pills in her hand that day, and before long she and Pastor Sam were renewed in their faith. When God finally allowed Erby to speak and instruct Gloria in the ways of God, Gloria was healed of her disease.

Gloria Phillips went on to become a much sought-after Bible teacher, and she continues her teaching ministry today. Gloria gives credit and thanks to Erby, her faithful household helper, who persevered for four difficult years—praying, fasting, warring against the devil and believing God for her healing.[3] The integrity of Erby's Christian walk spoke loud and clear to the Phillips's household, even when she was silent.

While abstaining from all food for a season is the primary means of fasting, some cannot go completely without food for medical reasons. But there are many different ways to fast:

- Eat no solid food from sunup to sundown.
- Eat only vegetables and clear liquids.
- Take only bread and water.
- Take only clear liquids with no solid food.
- Drink only water.
- Abstain from all meat and/or "pleasant food" (Dan. 10:2-3, *NKJV*).
- Follow the "Esther fast," taking no food or water for three days (see Esther 4:16).

• Abstain from sweets or certain favorite foods or activities for a season, while giving more time to prayer.

We suggest that you seek the Lord's guidance as to the type and length of fast you pursue, but beginning with shorter periods before attempting a prolonged fast is advisable. It is also advisable to consult your doctor before beginning any fast. The point is that fasting, in whatever form, allows you to concentrate on prayer and Scripture. Often the Holy Spirit will speak to you through the Word to give correction or encouragement, as well as give you strategy for the battles you are facing.

Treasures of Darkness

While fasting is a discipline many Christians choose to ignore, there is another discipline that none of us can ignore: hardship and adversity. Paul wrote to Timothy: "You therefore must endure hardship as a good soldier of Jesus Christ. No one engaged in warfare entangles himself with the affairs of this life, that he may please him who enlisted him as a soldier" (2 Tim. 2:3-4, *NKJV*).

During a difficult period in my own life several years ago, I (Ruthanne) developed the habit of walking a mile every day to talk to the Lord and settle my thoughts. I was dealing with a rebellious teenager, caring for my invalid in-laws living in our home, and trying to cope with financial pressures and myriad problems while my husband traveled frequently. I struggled against self-pity and the feeling that I was shouldering the load alone.

On my walk one crisp October morning, the Lord spoke to me through Isaiah 45:3: "I will give you the treasures of darkness, riches stored in secret places, so that you may know that I am the LORD, the God of Israel, who summons you by name."

Then He said very clearly, "Ruthanne, these are precious days. I am teaching you the treasures of darkness."

I desperately wanted God to quickly solve all these problems— they certainly didn't seem "precious" to my natural mind. Yet I knew they weren't going to evaporate overnight. The Lord said He was teaching me as I allowed Him to—there was value in the experience. Then I remembered reading about Jesus that "although he was a son, he learned obedience from what he suffered" (Heb. 5:8).

After that morning with the Lord under the oak trees, my circumstances actually got worse, not better. But I began to see that from God's point of view, my response to the difficulties was more important than the problems themselves. He obviously wanted to change me, and I finally yielded to His plan.

I have come to believe that God does His best work in darkness: in creation, in the Incarnation, in the Garden of Gethsemane, at Calvary, in my own "dark night of the soul."

The glory of it all for me was not just seeing circumstances change. (They eventually did, though not in all the ways I had hoped for.) The greater blessing was allowing God to change me. And in the process I came to know God and His character and faithfulness as only adversity can teach. In fact, it was during those years that I learned my most valuable lessons about the principles of spiritual warfare.

The Battle of the Mind

"We demolish arguments and every pretension that sets itself up against the knowledge of God, and we take captive every thought to make it obedient to Christ" (2 Cor. 10:5).

All who enter the arena of spiritual warfare quickly learn that their mind is a battleground bombarded with doubt, discouragement, false accusations, and mockery from Satan and his emissaries. But we can ask the Holy Spirit to empower us to take captive our false thoughts and to make them obedient to Christ.

Ann, who was active with an effective ministry of counseling, deliverance and teaching, learned firsthand how the enemy assaults our minds. Because of her parents' advanced age and failing health, she had to pull back from public ministry to care for them. Although she knew this was God's plan for her, it was a difficult adjustment and she had to learn to discipline her mind.

"As time passed, I began to have more and more negative thoughts about everything—but especially about myself," she said. "I believed every 'tear down' thought that wandered past. It seemed I couldn't trust myself to hear the Lord, and every negative Scripture in the Word seemed aimed at me. Down and down I went. No longer any balance—just negative.

"I was finally fighting thoughts attacking my salvation. I couldn't pray, couldn't read the Word—and I didn't want to. Then one night the Lord told me to write a list of the good things about myself. I explained I had none, but He assured me He would show me this was untrue. And He began to give me the list.

"I argued every point in the beginning. For example, He said I had compassion. I could only feel the hardness of my heart. He went on to remind me of instances where I had shown compassion for Mom.

"As we went on I had a thought: Satan stands before the throne accusing believers [see Rev. 12:10]. So that gives new meaning to the Scripture that tells us to think on the good things [see Phil. 4:8]. The good report is needed to balance the thrusts of the wicked one, for oneself as well as for others.

"The Lord showed me that the mind is a battlefield. Enemy ammunition flies around, and we must learn to avoid it. If you caress it and claim it, it's yours. It is wise to counterattack with your own ammunition—the list of good things God has spoken to you, in addition to the written Word. Knowing that the Lord has given us spiritual weapons is so powerful for the tearing down of strongholds.

"When the enemy returns, I can say, 'Satan, the Lord says I do have compassion. I'll not receive the lies you are telling me.' This has released me. Now I feel more comfortable going to the Word, not because I have to (which leads to guilt) but because the desire is there. Now I can more quickly smile, and I walk with less of a burden."

The assignment God gave Ann was not an easy one, but in the end it led to the salvation of both her parents. How grateful she was that she had obeyed.

Unto the Glory of God

As we submit to these disciplines of prayer, fasting, patience in hardship, and controlling our thoughts, we truly can become women warriors empowered by the Holy Spirit. And all that we do will be to the glory of God our Father.

Our friend Lou shared the struggle she had to discipline her tongue. Her elderly mother had moved from another city to the apartment behind Lou's house. In her difficult adjustment to new surroundings and attending a different church, Lou's mother would often vent her frustrations on Lou.

"Well, everyone doesn't teach Sunday School for the right reasons," she said testily one day when Lou was talking about plans for her next lesson.

"Mother, I get the message," Lou snapped and then walked out of the room.

A few days later she shared the experience with her prayer partner, Nita, as they worked on plans for a church reception. "I know I need to control my tongue," Lou groaned, "but Mom's criticism just sets me off."

"When you said what you did, you received her message as if it were true," Nita reminded her. "You need to cancel those words and speak the truth instead. Let's go for a prayer walk while you begin to declare, 'I can do all things unto the glory of God.'"

As Lou made her declaration, she and Nita walked to the church fellowship hall to continue their planning. Upon entering the building, the first thing they saw was a dedication plaque on the wall with a large inscription: "Unto the glory of God."

"There's your confirmation," Nita said laughing. "You just need to remember to keep declaring it!"

Training That Molds

"What is the most important thing you have learned through your experiences in spiritual warfare?" we asked a number of seasoned intercessors.

Many responded, "Discipline"—that quality so essential to victory but so distasteful to the flesh. Who doesn't want to win in a skirmish with the enemy? Yet few of us easily submit to the discipline and dying to self that are necessary to overcome Satan's onslaughts.

"The enemy can use our own ignorance against us," one intercessor responded. "He knows the law that will bring accusations to those who are trying to live up to its standard. We must discipline ourselves to learn God's Word and use it as a weapon against the attacks of the enemy."

"Probably the most significant lesson I learned was the importance of disciplining my tongue—no gossip, backbiting, silly talk, coarse jesting," another wrote. "In prayer and warfare, we should use our tongues according to the Word of God and allow the Holy Spirit to lead us in what we say to other people."

"I must always be prepared, try never to let my guard down," a third person said, "and listen continually for the voice of the Holy Spirit."

Anyone who has gone through conventional military training will tell you that discipline, obedience and persistence are critically important in producing a successful soldier. The same principles apply to our spiritual training.

Webster defines "discipline" as "training that corrects, molds, or perfects the mental faculties or moral character." Our yielding to the correcting, molding and perfecting work of the Holy Spirit can be painful, but it pays rich dividends by making us effective spiritual warriors.

Many modern-day Esthers and Annas have come to their "royal positions" for such a time as this. Discipline and balance—doing what we need to do to cooperate with God—are hallmarks of Spirit-empowered women. These are the women who successfully use the weapons of and effective strategies for spiritual warfare, which is our next topic.

Prayer

Lord, I thank You for teaching us to pray specifically and with persistence, assuring us that when we ask, You hear. Help me to be disciplined, tenacious and faithful in prayer, always sensitive to the Holy Spirit's leading. Lord, forgive me for expecting You to answer according to my wishes and timetable. Help me to trust Your perfect timing, for I know You never make a mistake.
Thank You for Your great faithfulness! Amen.

Our Weapons and Strategy

For though we live in the world, we do not wage war as the world does.
The weapons we fight with are not the weapons of the world. On the
contrary, they have divine power to demolish strongholds.

2 CORINTHIANS 10:3-4

Put on God's whole armor . . . that you may be able successfully to stand
up against [all] the strategies and the deceits of the devil.

EPHESIANS 6:11, *AMP*

"In the name of Jesus, you give that purse back to me," Kay shouted
as she chased a young teenager across the grocery-store parking lot.
"I earned that money, and you have no right to it."

As Kay grabbed the scared kid by the arm and jerked her purse
out of his hand, he broke down crying. It was his first time to try
purse snatching as he'd seen his older buddies do. But he picked
the wrong young woman in this case—or the right one, depending
on how you looked at it.

Kay knows she has authority in the name of Jesus, and she instinctively responded to the challenge without thinking of the possible dangers. She began sharing the gospel with the youngster, explaining that he needed to accept Jesus as Savior and then trust God to provide him a job. He walked away visibly shaken.

"Kay, you could have gotten hurt!" I (Ruthanne) said when she shared the incident. A convert from the drug culture, Kay was attending Bible school where my husband was a teacher. The store where she had stopped was a known trouble spot for thievery.

"I had just gotten paid at work, and I needed that money to pay my school bill," she said. "No way was I going to let the devil steal from me!"

It was no surprise that Kay went on to become a missionary in Asia, where for more than 30 years God has used her to do damage to Satan's kingdom. She now pastors two churches and has a daily television ministry in her nation.

The Name of Jesus

We've already established that our conflict is with an invisible enemy and his evil agents in the spiritual realm, operating through individuals. We cannot use physical artillery against such enemies, but God has given us invisible spiritual weapons. In fact, they truly are weapons of mass destruction!

In the just-related purse-snatching story, Kay used one of the primary weapons, the name of Jesus. To unbelievers all over the world, the name of Jesus is a common curse word—though you never hear the name of any false religion's founder used as a curse word. Surely this is because all false religions come from the same source: Satan.

For you to use the name of Jesus with authority, of course you must be in right relationship with Him. Consider these Scriptures:

> You are my King and my God. . . . Through you we push back our enemies; through your name we trample our foes (Ps. 44:4-5).

The seventy-two returned with joy and said, "Lord, even the demons submit to us in your name." He replied . . . "I have given you authority to trample on snakes and scorpions and to overcome all the power of the enemy; nothing will harm you" (Luke 10:17-19).

They overcame him [Satan] by the blood of the Lamb and by the word of their testimony (Rev. 12:11).

The only way to use the name of Jesus as a weapon is to speak to the enemy, as Jesus did in the wilderness (see Luke 4:4,8,12). As Paul Billheimer notes, we should not feel reticent about speaking to the evil powers of darkness:

Many believers have been so tyrannized and dominated by Satan and the prevailing theology of Satan's power and invincibility that, like me, they would never dare to speak directly to him, even in the name of Jesus. For years, I couldn't imagine Satan running away. . . . When I mustered enough courage to speak directly to him in the name of Jesus, it was a great surprise to me to discover an immediate sense of deliverance—as though he had vanished, melted away. . . .

The only way we can be sure that he knows we are resisting him is to *speak aloud*, to directly and audibly confront him with the truth.

May I remind you again that *our resistance* by itself is not what causes Satan to flee; he flees because of the *power of Jesus* which is ours through prayer.[1]

Bible teacher Dean Sherman expands on this thought:

Man . . . has authority; based on what Christ did on the Cross and through His resurrection. Man can still employ Satan through selfishness and sin, but the balance of power on the earth rests with man in the name of Jesus Christ. The authority is complete in man as long as man is in relationship with God through Jesus Christ. With our authority comes the responsibility to use it for God's purposes. If we don't rebuke the devil, he will not be rebuked. If we don't drive him back, he will not leave. It is up to us. Satan knows of our authority, but hopes we will stay ignorant.

We must be as convinced of our authority as the devil is.[2]

The Blood of Jesus

The sacrificial death, burial and resurrection of Jesus are the basis of our victory over Satan. In order to redeem us, Jesus had to come to earth in human form, as Hebrews declares: "Since the children have flesh and blood, he too shared in their humanity so that by his death he might destroy him who holds the power of death—that is, the devil—and free those who all their lives were held in slavery by their fear of death" (Heb. 2:14-15).

When we confess our sins and repent—meaning to *turn* from sin—the blood of Jesus cleanses us and puts us in right relationship with God. We call it being born again. Once we have this experience, we are not only protected by the blood of Jesus, but we are also authorized to use the blood as a weapon of warfare. H. A. Maxwell Whyte says:

> The destroyer cannot get in under the Blood-line where it has been placed. But, unfortunately, too many have been loosely taught that "Satan cannot get through the Blood-line." They have not been informed that *Satan can and does get through if the Blood-line is let down*. And how do we let it down? *By disobedience.*
>
> We can hardly claim to be under the Blood of Jesus if we are walking in deliberate disobedience. . . . Sprinkling of the Blood of Jesus without obedience to the Word of God will avail us nothing.[3]

To "plead the blood of Jesus" means to appropriate our Savior's shed blood as protection from the evil one. The practice is based on the Passover, when the blood of a lamb was applied to the doorposts and lintel of every Jewish home, protecting the inhabitants from the death angel who would pass through Egypt and take the oldest male of every family. The angel passed over those homes that were under the blood (see Exod. 12:1-13).

Of course, the blood of lambs and other animals was a temporary solution for sin. Only the shedding and appropriating of the blood of Jesus provided a permanent atonement. Whyte writes:

In the natural world, we would have no difficulty understanding how to apply disinfectant to an infection. We would take the disinfectant and sprinkle or pour it upon the infection, and the result would be that all germs and living organisms present in that infection would die.

Now we should have no difficulty in doing the same thing spiritually. Wherever Satan is at work, we must apply the only corrective antidote there is—the Blood of Jesus. There is absolutely no alternative, no substitute. Prayer, praise, worship, and devotion all have their part in our approach to God; but the Blood of Jesus is the only effective counteragent to corruption.

This is why Satan has always tried to take the Blood out of our churches. If there is no disinfectant, then his demons are free to continue their deadly work of destruction in spirit, soul, and body. . . .

In every situation where you sense that you are under the attack of Satan or needing special protection, that is the time to plead the Blood. By so doing, you are reminding God that you are trusting in His mercy; you are reminding Satan that he cannot touch you as long as you are under the Blood; and you are reminding yourself of the ground of your confidence in Christ![4]

The Power of the Blood

I (Ruthanne) learned in a dramatic way the power of the blood of Jesus as a weapon. Years ago, my husband, John, went on a mission outreach to Haiti with a group of his students. One Sunday afternoon, he joined two other missionaries to drive to a remote village church up a mountain outside Port-au-Prince. To get there they left the main road, drove on a small "goat track" road, and then parked the jeep and walked the rest of the way.

As John drove on the return trip, he inched up the small road to reach the main road but was unable to see over the nose of the jeep because of the incline. Suddenly, he realized that the right front wheel had gone off the road. The missionary in the front seat immediately cried out, "The blood of Jesus! The blood of Jesus! The blood of Jesus!"

By all the laws of physics, the jeep should have crashed to the valley several hundred feet below. Instead, it surged upward, spanned a gap between the road and a boulder, and stopped. The front differential rested on a rock on the other side of the gap; the left rear wheel was the only wheel on solid ground.

John and the missionaries climbed out of the jeep on the uphill side and had a thanksgiving service in the middle of the road. At that moment, the pastor John had preached for that morning drove up in his small truck. "I was praying for you and had a feeling I needed to come check on you," he said. A group of students were with him, and they helped maneuver the jeep onto the main road, so they could tow it down the mountain.

As they drove on, they came upon a group of men carrying a Haitian's body from a ravine below up to the roadside. He had been killed when his car had gone off the road about the same time as John's near brush with death.

"It seemed a malevolent spirit was determined to kill someone on that road, and he took revenge on someone with no divine protection," John reported. "After I returned to Dallas, an intercessor friend told me the Holy Spirit had given her and a group of students a burden to pray for my safety on that trip. They had prayed fervently two weeks before I'd even left; the Holy Spirit showed her that the devil would try to kill me in Haiti. Later a missionary friend told me the road has a voodoo curse on it, and a certain number of people are killed on it every year. Thank God for obedient intercessors, the power of prayer and the protection of the blood of Jesus!"

Arthur Mathews declares, "The only man [or woman] who can keep the enemy at bay is the intercessor, and blessed is that intercessor who knows how to use the power of the blood in spiritual warfare."[5]

Praise as a Weapon

"Jehoshaphat appointed men to sing to the LORD and to praise him for the splendor of his holiness as they went out at the head of the army. . . . As they began to sing and praise, the LORD set ambushes against the men . . . who were invading Judah, and they were defeated" (2 Chron. 20:21-22).

Praise has a threefold purpose in spiritual warfare:

1. It glorifies God and keeps our focus on Him and His power.
2. It terrifies the enemy and throws his ranks into confusion.
3. It encourages the believer as he or she proclaims the victory in the spiritual realm before it is manifested in the natural realm.

Walking in a spirit of praise helps us remember that we fight from a position of victory, not defeat (see Eph. 1:18-23). Often circumstances look totally bleak just as we are on the threshold of a breakthrough, because the enemy hurls his worst shot just before his defeat is sealed. Therefore, it is always too soon to quit!

Scripture says that "His [God's] way is in the whirlwind and the storm, and clouds are the dust of his feet" (Nah. 1:3b). Arthur Mathews reminds us that "Nowhere is the greatness of God seen to such advantage as it is in His ability to use as His chariot of conquest the circumstances that pose the greatest threat to His cause."[6]

Strategy Lessons

Paul warned the early Christians to stand against the devil's "wiles," or strategies (Eph. 6:11, *NKJV*). Strategy is the science and art of conducting a military campaign on a broad scale. A military commander sets the goal for the campaign and then devises methods for achieving it. Tactics are the specific methods he or she employs to fulfill the strategy, based upon reports from intelligence agents and surveillance equipment.

If the devil has schemes, or military strategies, then we certainly need God's strategy for the specific battles He calls us to fight. The Holy Spirit is the intelligence agent who knows the enemy's strategy and tactics; it is critical that we seek His guidance and fight our battles accordingly.

As a young Christian, I (Quin) thought I could fight every giant, pray for every troubled marriage, intercede for any problem—whether people asked for prayer or not! Soon exhausted, I learned mainly by trial and error that not every battle is mine, and not every battle strategy is the same. We cannot standardize spiritual warfare, as Scripture makes clear.

We see many different battle plans in Scripture. David learned to inquire of the Lord, "Shall I go to battle?" Sometimes the Lord would say yes, and sometimes He would give different instructions. Once He told David to wait until he heard "the sound of marching in the tops of the mulberry trees" (2 Sam. 5:24, *NKJV*)!

When I'm seeking God's guidance for a strategy, I use what I call a Four-W strategy: Worship-Wait-Word-Warfare. I *worship* the Lord; then I *wait* in His presence until He quickens something in

His *Word* to use in *warfare* against the enemy in the battle at hand.

My "quiet time" isn't always quiet: I like to pray aloud, shout, stamp my feet, laugh and clap. At other times I may be very quiet, praying silently with hands uplifted, bowing, kneeling or lying prostrate on the floor.

I sometimes shout *before* I've seen any signs of victory, just as the Israelites did before the walls of Jericho collapsed. God's battle plan called for them to march for six days in silence and on the seventh day shout aloud at the sound of the trumpet. We may need to raise such a battle cry, or shout, as part of our spiritual warfare strategy, as these verses indicate:

> Clap your hands, all you nations; shout to God with cries of joy (Ps. 47:1).

> Sing, O Daughter of Zion; shout aloud, O Israel! Be glad and rejoice with all your heart, O Daughter of Jerusalem! The LORD has . . . turned back your enemy (Zeph. 3:14-15a).

Our mouths are our most effective means of using our spiritual weapons. God says His Word will not return void (see Isa. 55:11), so I use my tongue to praise Him and to war against demonic power.

He Trains My Hands for War

David wrote, "Praise be to the LORD, my Rock, who trains my hands for war, my fingers for battle" (Ps. 144:1). I often use my hands in warfare intercession. When I did a word study on the hand, I discovered many Scriptures related to God's hand and warfare:

> Your right hand, O LORD, was majestic in power. Your right hand, O LORD, shattered the enemy (Exod. 15:6).

> His right hand and His holy arm have gained Him the victory (Ps. 98:1b, *NKJV*).

For I am the LORD, your God, who takes hold of your right hand and says to you, Do not fear; I will help you (Isa. 41:13).

One form of the Hebrew word for "hand" means "open hand," while another form means "closed hand." In prayer I extend my open hand to the Lord, beseeching Him on behalf of the person I'm interceding for. In warfare I close my other hand into a fist and shake it at Satan, declaring the Word of God on behalf of the one for whom I'm battling.

I also clap my hands loudly. I see two reasons for this in the Bible: to praise the Lord and to mock God's enemy (see Ps. 47:1-2; Lam. 2:15).

This is what the Sovereign LORD says: Strike your hands together and stamp your feet and cry out "Alas!" because of all the wicked and detestable practices of the house of Israel (Ezek. 6:11).

So then, son of man, prophesy and strike your hands together. Let the sword strike twice, even three times (Ezek. 21:14a).

Striking my hands together, I may say, "You spirit of discouragement, be gone! You have no place in this home, which is dedicated to the Lord God of hosts."

Still clapping, I applaud the Lord: "Thank You, Lord, for Your spirit of peace. I applaud You, for You are on the throne as king of my life and my home. Nothing is impossible for You, Lord!"

One intercessor uses her tambourine in spiritual warfare, symbolically striking the enemy as she strikes the instrument with her hand. God gave us a body and creative ways to praise Him with it—as well as ways to use it in warfare against His enemy. So our prayer times need not be dull!

The Weapon of Joy

"The righteous will see and fear; they will laugh at him, saying, 'Here now is the man who did not make God his stronghold'" (Ps. 52:6-7b).

"The Virgin Daughter of Zion despises you and mocks you [Sennacherib, king of Assyria]. . . . Who is it you have insulted and blasphemed?" (2 Kings 19:21-22).

"Laugh" in the biblical sense includes the meanings "to mock, to play, to make sport, to deride, to laugh, to scorn." There is also a laugh that is merry, and it does our hearts good like a medicine (see Prov. 17:22).

David wrote, "When the Lord brought back the captives to Zion . . . our mouths were filled with laughter, our tongues with songs of joy" (Ps. 126:1a-2).

Examples of women in the Bible who rejoiced are Miriam (see Exod. 15:20-21), Hannah (see 1 Sam. 2:1-10) and Mary (see Luke 1:46-55). And Paul wrote, "Rejoice in the Lord always. I will say it again: Rejoice!" (Phil. 4:4).

Anne, a young Bible-school graduate, felt God's call to go on an African mission outreach, but she had no money for the trip. When she and her prayer partner prayed, the friend saw a vision of two bags falling at Anne's feet with the needed two thousand dollars. Uncontrollable laughter hit Anne.

"I am going to laugh my way to Africa," she told her praying friend. In just two days, all the money came in through unexpected ways. "I laughed at the devil while I was waiting for the money," she said, "because I knew he wasn't going to keep me from going on God's mission. I also laughed with joy over what God was going to accomplish."

Anne has since served the Lord in several nations, depending entirely on His provision. Today where she lives in Southeast Asia, she coordinates prayer for her nation by mobilizing prayer groups from many churches and denominations. And she's still laughing at the enemy!

Pray in Agreement

Jesus said, "If two of you on earth agree about anything you ask for, it will be done for you by my Father in heaven. For where two or three come together in my name, there am I with them" (Matt. 18:19-20). The prayer of agreement is a powerful strategy in spiritual warfare.

The word "agree" in Matthew 18:19 is based on a Greek root from which we get our English word "symphony." It means "to be in harmony or accord concerning a matter." We believe it is essential to have at least one specific friend—someone familiar with the current battles we're dealing with—to stand in agreement with us as prayer support. Such partners also provide a blanket of prayer for us when we're traveling, ministering—or writing a book!

Prayer partners play a spiritual role that is analogous to the army specialists who create a corridor of safety for the tanks and other armaments to be used to mount an offensive against the enemy. These soldiers detonate land mines, clear barbed-wire entanglements, bulldoze man-made barriers and build emergency bridges, so that the army can invade enemy territory. Prayer partners often pray in advance to help neutralize the enemy's forces.

Individual prayer and warfare is important, but interceding with a prayer partner or a group of believers strengthens the prayer's effectiveness. There is strength in numbers! If the two of you or the entire group is fasting in unity, the warfare is even stronger.

First we should ask the Lord *how* He wants us to pray. Then in agreement, *with one mind*, we pray as He directs, persisting with our prayer partners until we see results.

Bind the Strongman

Jesus gave us His authority over the devil and his evil cohorts, yet to see results, we must be motivated to use that authority. Consider what He taught His followers: "I will give you the keys of the kingdom of heaven; whatever you bind on earth will be bound in heaven, and whatever you loose on earth will be loosed in heaven" (Matt. 16:19).

He also said, "No one can enter a strong man's house and plunder his goods, unless he first binds the strong man, and then he will plunder his house" (Mark 3:27, *NKJV*).

To bind evil spirits means to restrain their movement by addressing them directly and forbidding them to continue their destructive activity. Through the power of the Holy Spirit, our words loose the person from the enemy's bondage. In prayer we ask the Holy Spirit to minister to his or her need. Our prayer is directed to God, our warfare at the enemy. This tactic of binding evil spirits is especially effective when praying in agreement with a prayer partner.

Renee learned to use this important tactic one day when she went to visit her nineteen-year-old son. Not finding him at home, she went on in and was shocked at the mess she found. She thoroughly cleaned the apartment, cooked a meal and then washed all the dirty clothes lying around.

While putting things in order, Renee found a gun Mike had stolen from her policeman husband, Mike's stepfather. It had one bullet in it. Realizing that Mike was intent on shooting himself, she began to do spiritual battle for her son's life.

"Thank You, Lord, for giving us authority to use Your name to set captives free," she declared. "I plead the blood of Jesus over Mike and ask You to protect his life. I come against the strong man of rejection operating against my son and bind Your power in Jesus' name. I bind all spirits of rejection, hate, anger, murder and suicide, in Jesus' name. I bind all unclean spirits associated with drug abuse, and I cut Mike loose from past hurts and from unhealthy relationships. I command the spirits that are blinding and controlling him to release him, in Jesus' name.

"Lord, let Your peace permeate this apartment. Show Mike how much You love him and desire to set him free from the bondage of the enemy. Thank You, Lord, for protecting his life and drawing him into fellowship with You."

Renee sang and filled the place with praises to the Lord as she cooked and cleaned. Before leaving, she posted a note: "Mike—I did this today because I love you. No strings attached. Mom."

Seven difficult years passed before Mike finally came to Renee and asked her to pray for his deliverance, but at last he was set free. "If I hadn't fought for Mike and kept showing him unconditional love, I don't think my son would still be alive," she said. "But he is alive, and he's serving the Lord with his wife and children."

Sometimes the strong man that needs binding is readily discerned; at other times it is less obvious. We must depend on the Holy Spirit in every situation to reveal appropriate strategy and empower us to get the job done. In the next chapter, we will look at the things that give the enemy access to us.

Prayer

*Thank You, Father, for the spiritual weapons You provide
and the wisdom You give for using them effectively. Help me
always to depend upon Your strength in every battle and never to
lean on my own understanding. Lord, I want to be a spiritual
warrior who remains faithful until victory comes and You receive
the honor and glory. In Jesus' name, amen.*

An Open Door to the Enemy

You shall have no other gods before or besides Me. You shall not make yourself any graven image. . . . You shall not bow down yourself to them or serve them; for I the Lord your God am a jealous God, visiting the iniquity of the fathers upon the children to the third and fourth generation of those who hate Me, but showing mercy and steadfast love to a thousand generations of those who love Me and keep My commandments.

EXODUS 20:3-6, *AMP*

Pauline was a compulsive buyer, addicted to shopping. She had credit cards for most major department stores in Atlanta and used one nearly every time she went into a store. She couldn't resist buying something—clothes, knickknacks, appliances, furniture, gifts. For Pauline, shopping was more than a hobby. It took precedence over other priorities—it became an idol. "It's how I got my kicks," she says.

When Pauline heard a Christian teacher speak on family generational weaknesses, she suddenly realized that her father was addicted to alcohol, but she and her sister were obsessive shoppers. It was a different "substance" but the same compulsive behavior pattern.

Following the teacher's suggestions, Pauline confessed her sin and asked the Lord to forgive her. Then to break the habit's control over her, she declared aloud: "Satan, you will no longer have a foothold in my life by making me greedy for things I don't need. I renounce this idol and declare the stronghold broken by the authority of Jesus Christ. I recognize this bondage of generational weakness, and by the blood of Jesus I sever it."

Then she prayed, "Heavenly Father, I yield to You in this area, trusting You that this bondage is removed from my life. Thank You that by the power of the Holy Spirit and according to Your Word, I can and will walk in obedience to You and in victory. I make You, and You only, the Lord of my life. In Jesus' name, amen."

Pauline and her husband had several counseling sessions with their pastor. She also destroyed all of her credit cards as an outward sign that she would walk in her deliverance and keep her focus on Jesus.

Our Spiritual Heritage

What is the origin of such a compulsive-addictive behavior? What about other problems such as uncontrollable anger, fear of crowds, rebellion, or chronic illness? How is it that the enemy has access to us as Christians?

Unfortunately there is no pat answer, for various factors are involved in such problems. And according to Exodus 20:3-6, we can find one of these factors in our family tree. God says that the serious sin of idolatry will have repercussions upon future generations. Just as our genetic heritage determines what our physical characteristics will be, so our *spiritual heritage* bears strongly on our behavioral tendencies, both positive and negative.

The iniquity of the forefathers brings a curse upon the family line—it opens a door to the enemy. This word "iniquity" does not mean individual sinful acts; it means "perverseness" and comes from a Hebrew root meaning "to be bent or crooked."[1] The word implies a basic attitude of rebellion, plus the consequences that iniquity produces. We see the same word in the prophecy concerning Jesus the Messiah: "The LORD has laid on him the *iniquity* of us all" (Isa. 53:6, emphasis added). Jesus bore the cumulative sinfulness of humankind.

We are not accountable for our forefathers' individual acts of sin; we have plenty of our own for which we are responsible. And Galatians 3:13 declares that Jesus became "a curse for us," providing a means for our deliverance. But we do inherit a susceptibility to sin in the same areas that troubled our forefathers. We tend to be bent, or crooked (weak), in the same places—as Pauline's case illustrates. Our enemy is not omniscient, but he knows where these weak areas are, because his agents have been working against our family members and all humankind for generations.

We see such sin patterns in families all the time, including the families in the Bible. Look at Abraham, the patriarch we laud as a godly example. On two occasions he lied about his wife, Sarah, calling her his sister. Then Abraham's son Isaac lied about his wife, Rebekah, saying she was his sister. Isaac's son Jacob deceived him so that he could receive the blessing due the firstborn, Esau. Then Jacob's sons deceived him about his son Joseph, causing him to grieve for years. The tendency to lie and deceive showed up in succeeding generations, each time causing more serious consequences.

King David's besetting sin was his adultery with Bathsheba. Sexual sin also became a problem with his sons. Finally, because his son Solomon took hundreds of foreign wives and began to worship their false gods, God took the kingdom from him. The gravity of Solomon's sin was even greater than that of his father, David.

Sins That Bring Curses

We read in Deuteronomy chapters 27 and 28 that curses are promised for sins in these six areas: idolatry, dishonoring of parents, dishonesty and deception, cruelty to the helpless, sexual sin of any kind, and disregard for the law.[2]

Pastor Burton Stokes writes:

> There is that unseen and mysterious connection between a father's sins and the path of his children. If the father commits certain kinds of sin, his offspring are prone to the same kinds of sin, regardless of their training, or the social, cultural, and environmental influences on them. . . . Sin is committed and iniquity is "passed down" to the children, to the third and fourth generation. . . . Each generation adds to the cumulative iniquity; further weakening the resistance of the next generation.[3]

We do not mean to imply that there is any deficiency in the power of the blood of Jesus, which redeems us from the curse of sin, or that believers today are bound to the letter of Old Testament law. But if we rebel in our hearts and build idols in our lives, we can be ensnared again by the same yoke of bondage from which we've been delivered (see Gal. 5:1,16). Thus we again become susceptible to the curse.

Bible teacher Derek Prince writes:

> Sometimes curses may not have their origin in previous generations. They may be the result of deeds or events in your own lifetime. Or it may be that a curse from previous generations has been compounded by things you yourself have done. . . . Christians who are undisciplined, disobedient, and out of harmony forfeit their claim on God's protection.[4]

These insights are not intended to bring us into fear or bondage, nor cause us to attribute every problem, habit or bad character trait to a curse or a demon. Emotional and behavioral problems sometimes have a physiological or biological basis. For instance, premenstrual women often have fluctuating blood-sugar levels that trigger and intensify symptoms such as exhaustion, depression, anxiety, irritability, headaches, dizziness and mood swings. And menopause sometimes causes the same symptoms, in addition to annoying hot flashes. Certainly prayer is always appropriate, but some of these problems may also call for treatment by diet modification, hormone supplements or vitamin therapy. We recommend asking the Lord for guidance in these matters, and if the Lord so directs, consult a doctor.

Looking at the various factors involved with behavior problems helps us to become aware of our vulnerabilities, to renounce the sins we've yielded to in our areas of weakness, and then with the help of the Holy Spirit to strengthen our defenses against the evil one.

The Danger of Idolatry

Though God strictly forbade Israel to engage in any form of idol worship, His people rebelled against Him. They committed spiritual adultery as they took up their neighbors' evil ways of idolatry. As a result, God removed His protection, allowing their enemies to capture and enslave them. McCandlish Phillips explains the gravity of this sin:

> Satan lusts for worship. Because it belongs exclusively to God, he desires it for himself. He would rather have worship than anything else. . . . He sets up many objects as alternatives to the worship of God. This is idolatry in the crudest form. . . .
>
> Satan stands behind every image and every idol, receiving as unto himself the worship, the respect, and adoration that is directed to them, which belongs only to the living God. . . . The cumulative effect of idols and images is to bring a curse upon the land.[5]

Over the many years I (Ruthanne) traveled overseas with my late husband, I observed that the areas of the world filled with idols and false religions are generally among the poorest and most disease-ridden nations on earth. John and I became more keenly aware of the need for prayer coverage and God's protection when we would travel in those areas. In fact, I began sending my prayer partners details about our itinerary and ministry schedule so they could pray specifically for us—and their prayers helped make a difference on many of our trips.

Protected by the Blood of Jesus

Once on a trip to India, our intended host had become ill, so we were guests of a family who were nominal Christians. Hideous images of Hindu gods hung on the walls of our room, but we were too blurry from jet lag and 36 hours of travel to give them more than a passing glance as we fell into bed. In the middle of the night, fireworks celebrating a Hindu festival awakened us. A sudden wave of nausea swept over me, and my head throbbed with pain. Sensing an evil presence emanating from those images in the room, I began to bind the spirits of bondage, oppression and the Antichrist, and to plead the blood of Jesus over myself.

My husband commanded all evil spirits to leave and then he prayed for my healing. We dedicated that room to God for the week of our visit, and for the next five hours we played tapes of praise and worship music. After resting and recuperating the next day, I was able to keep my speaking engagement. But the entire time we traveled around India on that trip was a spiritual battle.

I don't believe our host family gave credence to those graven images on the guest-room walls; they probably just considered them a part of the room's decor. But the images gave the evil spirits a legal right to be present until we drove them away. In fact, the artisans who make such objects often do their work under demonic influence, and they invite the evil spirits to inhabit the objects. I believe I was vulnerable to attack because of fatigue, and I wasn't alert and attentive to the Holy Spirit.

We had a similar experience in Bali, Indonesia, a few years later. The boy who cleaned our hotel room every day gave us a carved figure as a gift on the day we left. We accepted it graciously and gave him the customary tip for his services. After arriving at our next stop, John and I both began having physical problems, and we quickly suspected that they had to do with that little statue. We learned it was the image of a Hindu warrior god. When we got rid of it, we both recovered!

People in Western cultures rarely bow down to images or idols, although the influx into this country of New Age and Eastern religious practices has made it more prevalent in recent years. But many New Testament references to idolatry equate this sin with rebellion, infidelity, immorality and other sins of the flesh (see Rom. 1:22-25; Gal. 4:8-9; Col. 3:5). One commentator writes:

> The modern believer must understand the vicious nature of idolatry. While we may not make or bow down to a statue, we must be constantly on guard that we let nothing come between us and God. As soon as anything does, that thing is an idol. In addition to material objects such as houses, land, and cars, idols can be people, popular heroes, or those whom we love. Objects of worship can even include things like fame, reputation, hobbies, pride, and deeds done in the name of the Lord. Idolatry is a dangerous and deceitful sin.[6]

Can a Christian Have a Demon?

Perhaps no other question has generated more debate and disagreement among Christians than whether a Christian can have a demon.

We firmly believe a Christian who is walking in right relationship to God cannot be possessed by a demon, as that would imply ownership, or total control. A Christian belongs to Christ, not the devil. But a believer who compromises with the enemy—falling into willful disobedience and idolatry—removes himself or herself from

God's protection. Such an individual certainly can be harassed and manipulated by demonic forces. But perhaps the greatest danger is that he or she is then open to being deceived by the enemy.

Dr. Ed Murphy, Bible teacher and former missionary, writes:

> Satan's goal is, through deception, to entice believers to sin or commit any act which quenches the Holy Spirit in their lives and/or to lessen their effectiveness in glorifying God through both personal conduct and Christian service. His desire is to find any area of our lives to which he can attach himself (Eph. 4:27). Through his demons he seeks to find any *sin handles* which give him the right to influence us into actions of disobedience to God. [7]

Dr. Murphy goes on to suggest three main doors through which demons exert influence over a human being:

> The first door is *at birth*. Some Christians were born demonized. This is often called by different names such as generational sin, familial sin, demonic transference, demonic inheritance, or the law of the inheritance of evil.
>
> The second door to demonize Christians is *through child abuse*, in at least four possible areas—sexual, physical, psychological, and spiritual.
>
> Spiritual child abuse . . . can occur when a child involuntarily receives demonic psychic/occult powers that are passed down through the family line. It can also occur when a child is voluntarily subjected to a spirit ceremony with the purpose of passing demonic psychic or occult spirits into his body. It can also occur when a curse is placed on a child by a malevolent spiritual practitioner, or by an angry person operating in the spirit realm. . . .
>
> The third door . . . is through his or her own willful sinful actions in childhood, youth, or adulthood. This usually

occurs in the realms of sexuality, occult, and destructive interpersonal relationships. Sin has been the scourge of humanity since the Fall. With sin comes demons. . . . Increased demonic activity and increased sinfulness go together.[8]

To the degree we choose to obey God—allowing the Holy Spirit to renew our mind through God's Word—is the degree to which we can overcome Satan's efforts to ensnare us! Consider Peter, who after hearing Jesus say that He would be killed and then raised on the third day, declared, "Never, Lord! . . . This shall never happen to you!" (Matt. 16:22).

Jesus responded, "Get behind me, Satan! You are a stumbling block to me; you do not have in mind the things of God, but the things of men" (Matt. 16:23).

Peter had walked with the Lord all of His ministry years. Yet Jesus clearly implies that Satan was influencing this disciple to focus on what he wanted, not on God's plan. His perspective was both limited and selfish, just as ours often is. We can be thankful that Peter's wish did not prevail!

Then we read of Simon the sorcerer, who became a believer and was baptized under Philip's ministry in Samaria (see Acts 8:5-13). Later, when Peter and other apostles laid hands on the new converts and they received the Holy Spirit, Simon was impressed. He offered to pay them to give him that power, but Peter told him, "Your heart is all wrong in God's sight. For I see that you are in the gall of bitterness and a bond forged by iniquity" (Acts 8:21,23, *AMP*).

Although Simon had become a Christian, the bond to his occult past had not been broken. Yielding to Satan's influence upon his mind, Simon sought a way to draw acclaim to himself, as he had done before his conversion (see Acts 8:9-11). It appears Simon received the rebuke, as he asked Peter to pray for him, but the narrative about him ends here.

What about Judas? For three years he associated closely with Jesus almost daily. Yet Satan entered his heart and caused him to betray the Master (see John 13:21-27).

Longing to Be Free

In ministering to hundreds of people all over the world, we have seen countless examples of believers under demonic bondage to one degree or another. Many, until they receive teaching on this subject, are unable even to identify their problem clearly. They just know something is wrong. And they long to be free.

Once after I (Quin) had been teaching a Christian women's group how to pray for their families, a woman asked for prayer.

"If there's anything in me that is blocking prayer—and there must be because my prayer life is so lacking—I want to be free," she whispered.

I studied the woman's face and noticed a strange stare in her eyes.

"Is Jesus Christ your personal Lord?" I asked.

"Yes, for over 10 years," she nodded. "I love Him."

The Holy Spirit prompted me to ask, "Do you have an American Indian heritage? Or do you think a curse could have been sent against you?"

"My granddaddy was an Indian chief," she answered.

Before I could even begin to pray, she suddenly spun into an Indian dance, complete with war whoops and shrieks. Having never encountered such a demonic manifestation, I was numb with shock for a few moments. Then several of us gathered around her and began singing about the blood of Jesus.

Taking authority in the name of Jesus, we commanded the evil spirits to be silent. In moments the woman quieted down and began responding to our prayers. She declared any curses against her to be null and void by the power of Jesus Christ. She asked God's forgiveness for the sins of her forefathers and for her own sin, and she ordered all unclean spirits to depart, never to torment her again.

"I don't know exactly what happened to me tonight, but I feel so free," she said, smiling, after our prayer session. Some of the leaders in the group agreed to follow up and help her walk in her deliverance.

I can't say whether curses were said over her as a child growing up in her Indian family, whether a relative had dedicated her to a false god when she was a baby or whether she herself had opened the door to evil spirits. I can only report what happened that night when she was released from bondage to freely worship the Lord Jesus Christ: Her whole countenance changed before our eyes.

I (Ruthanne) remember hearing the testimony of a woman in Canada who came to Christ from a devout Buddhist background. As her relationship with the Lord deepened, she desired to learn more about prayer and to become an intercessor. But as she prayed to dedicate her life for this purpose, she sensed the Lord saying to her, "You have unclean hands." As she wept and asked for understanding, the Holy Spirit reminded her of the times she had burned joss sticks and worshiped idols in Buddhist temples. After repenting for the things she had done in ignorance and renouncing her idol worship, she became a strong intercessor. And of course she was effective in helping other people break free from an occultic past.

Whatever your spiritual history may be, God wants to move you to a higher level of effectiveness in prayer and spiritual warfare.

Discernment Needed

Why address this issue of doors being opened to the enemy? To help women overcome generational weaknesses and iniquities, break the cycles of bondage in themselves and in their families, and make their homes a spiritual refuge. Then they can move on to fulfill God's purposes for their lives and become powerful in spiritual warfare. Pauline, the addicted shopper, is just one of many we've interviewed who has been set free.

As we pray for our own family members or when we minister to others, we ask the Holy Spirit to bring to our attention any generational sin or other issues that need to be addressed. We have renounced infidelity, divorce, abuse, unforgiveness, addictions, rebellion, occult activity, membership in secret societies and other generational weaknesses as they have been revealed. Then we declare that all these doors are closed to the enemy and sealed by the blood of Jesus, and we thank God for His forgiveness and cleansing.

Now let's look at how to find the areas where doors have been opened to the enemy and go over the guidelines for closing them.

Prayer

Father, I come before You as Daniel did to confess and repent of my sin and the iniquity of my forefathers. Forgive us for the sins of idolatry, witchcraft, rebellion, immorality of any kind and all addictions [add anything the Holy Spirit prompts you to include]. By the power and authority of Jesus Christ, I declare that any satanic influence directed toward me or my family was defeated by Jesus' death on the cross, and this family is under the blood of Jesus. I revoke any generational curses and declare they will go no further. Jesus became a curse for us, and we are a generation that serves God.

Father, forgive us for depending upon any source besides You for peace and fulfillment. Pour out Your supernatural power in my family so that we will not be bound by the things of the natural world. Thank You that my children will take their place in the Body of Christ and fulfill Your calling upon their lives.

Lord, I submit to You, and my hope and expectations are from You alone [see Ps. 62:5, AMP]. Thank You for freeing us from the bondage of our past and cleansing us by the blood of Christ. Thank You for our positive heritage— for those ancestors who did follow You and prayed for us. Thank You for Your mercy and for the blessings You bestow upon me and my family. Amen.

8

Breaking Bondages

It is for freedom that Christ has set us free. Stand firm, then, and do not let yourselves be burdened again by a yoke of slavery.

GALATIANS 5:1

Ellen had been a Christian since childhood, but when things didn't go her way, she would verbally attack those who displeased her. She excused her temper by saying, "Well, I'm Irish, and everyone knows the Irish easily fly off the handle."

Ellen's father also had a problem with anger, so that was her particular negative spiritual heritage. It was a vulnerable area where the enemy took advantage, and becoming a Christian didn't eradicate her bad temper. She just made excuses for it. When the Lord spotlighted her problem, Ellen repented, renounced her sin of anger and speaking bitter words, and declared the bondage broken by the blood of Jesus.

"I had to see my anger for what it was—bondage to sin that was rooted in unforgiveness," she said. "Then I asked the Holy Spirit to put a guard on my tongue and alert me when I was in danger of falling into my old habit." Now Ellen gives attention to walking in an attitude of forgiveness, and she renews her mind with Scripture to keep the enemy from ensnaring her again.

Untold numbers of believers struggle with problems similar to Ellen's—or to Pauline's struggle with compulsive shopping mentioned in the previous chapter—that paralyze their spiritual growth. Such negative behavior and bondage is like a chain holding us to an area of weakness from our pre-Christian experience or to a vulnerable area from our negative spiritual heritage. It exists because a door has been opened, and we have given the enemy the right to enter. These bondages typically affect our mind, will and emotions. They in turn influence our behavior and result in angry reactions, rebellion, depression, threats of suicide, compulsive behavior, overeating, lying, stealing, sexual sin, substance addictions, and other destructive habits.

The apostle Paul addressed the problem of such bondages when he wrote to the church at Corinth, "I fear that there may be quarreling, jealousy, outbursts of anger, factions, slander, gossip, arrogance and disorder. I am afraid that when I come again my God will humble me before you, and I will be grieved over many who have sinned earlier and have not repented of the impurity, sexual sin and debauchery in which they have indulged" (2 Cor. 12:20b-21).

Many Christians struggling with these problems are leading defeated lives, burdened with guilt. They try to change their behavior on their own, only to fail and sink deeper into despair. It is only through repenting, forgiving themselves and others and allowing the Holy Spirit to renew their minds that they can be free from the chains that hold them. Before we discuss how to be free, however, we first need to examine some major areas of bondage:

- generational sin
- unforgiveness
- grief and disappointment
- addictions

- rejection and a negative self-image
- illicit sexual activity
- occult involvement

Because we have discussed generational sin in the previous chapter, we'll begin by examining the bondage brought about by unforgiveness.

Unforgiveness

Children in their naïveté sometimes express profound truth in the simplest of words—or even in made-up words. My (Ruthanne's) late husband came home from a weekend preaching trip once and shared part of a version of the Lord's Prayer from a pastor's young son: "Forgive us our trash-passes, as we forgive those who pass trash against us . . ."

To forgive means to give up the desire to get even or to "pass trash" against someone. It means to renounce anger and resentment, to release one's debtor. It is a decision made with the will, not based on emotions. We can *choose* to forgive the person who has offended us, whether we feel like it or not.

When we realize that any injustice we have suffered from another person is small compared to our own sin against God, the necessity to forgive others is put in proper perspective. In other words, the "trash" we've passed against our loving heavenly Father is much worse than all the "trash" others have passed against us!

The Lord's command is clear: "If you forgive men when they sin against you, your heavenly Father will also forgive you. But if you do not forgive men their sins, your Father will not forgive your sins" (Matt. 6:14).

Refusing to forgive the person who offended or hurt you creates an unhealthy bond between you and that person. Clinging to your resentment only increases your bitterness, poisons your relationships and makes life miserable. But when you choose to ask for God's help in forgiving the aggressor, that bondage is broken. Both parties are released, and the Holy Spirit then can bring healing and restoration. In fact, in some cases, a positive bonding in God's love can then take place.

Forgiving Sets You Free

The deeper the wound, the more essential forgiveness becomes, as Marie discovered. When her parents divorced shortly after her birth, a relative cared for her until her father remarried and brought her into his new home. The stepmother, unable to have children of her own, deeply resented Marie and was cruel to her. The forlorn little girl craved affection from her dad, but because of his drive to be successful in business, he was emotionally absent from her life.

Marie became promiscuous in her teen years as she sought love and acceptance, but soon the pain of repeated rejection made her wish to die. Then she began attending church with one of her dates, because it was the only way his parents would allow him to use the family car. For the first time, Marie heard the message of salvation in a way she'd not understood before. Over her boyfriend's protests, she stood up and asked Jesus to come into her heart, because she wanted assurance of going to heaven.

However, due to not being discipled in her faith, she soon fell into a worldly lifestyle when she went away to college. Her father got another divorce and remarried, widening the breach between them. Out of a sense of guilt, Marie felt responsible to take care of her new stepmother, who was an alcoholic and drug addict. In her despair, Marie called some Christians she had known years before and agreed to go to church with them.

That night she prayed, "Lord, if You will just forgive me, I'll serve You the rest of my life." As she lifted her hands in worship, she sensed the Lord say, "Marie, I've already forgiven you, and I love you."

Marie dropped out of college, began attending church regularly and in time met and married Mike, whose loving, Christian family was everything Marie's family was not. Although Mike's family loved and accepted her, Marie still longed for her own dad and the only mother she had ever known to love her as Mike's family loved him. Trying to ignore the broken area deep inside her, she became active in the church and enjoyed her two children and lovely home. "Yet my pain never went away," she told us.

Then the couple and their children moved to Mexico to work in a training program. With her happy façade firmly in place, Marie determined to serve the Lord there with her whole heart as she immersed herself in the needs of the people. But on the inside she was crying out for wholeness. Then someone mailed her a copy of the original edition of this book, and she read about the freedom that comes with forgiving.

"I'd always said that I forgave my father and stepmother, but I knew God was telling me to deal with my feelings on a deeper level," she said. "I realized that without Jesus, my behavior was no better than theirs, and I began to feel real love and empathy for both of them. I truly forgave them as I prayed that God's mercy and compassion would touch and change their lives and that He would give my dad a natural affection for me, his only child."

Only three days later Marie received a letter from her dad, written on the same day she had prayed her prayer of forgiveness. It had been mailed to a border town and brought into Mexico by one of her coworkers. The note read, "Dear Marie, here's a check. I was thinking about you today . . . thought you might need some money to get home." It didn't seem like much, but to Marie it was huge.

A few months later Marie went home to try to reach out to her dad. During her visit, the relationship with her father was healed as she heard words of love and approval from him for the first time in 34 years. "They were greater than gold," she told us. "At last I had received the miracle of my dad's love and his blessing. It was the beginning of a new life for me."

The truth is, we are *required* to forgive if we want to receive God's forgiveness and peace. When we recall Jesus' plea as He hung on the cross, "Father, forgive them, for they do not know what they are doing" (Luke 23:34), we are faced with our own sin and the need to free others by forgiving them. Gratitude for the mercy God extends to us, and a desire to demonstrate that gratefulness by obeying His Word, help us to forgive those who have wounded us.

Grief and Disappointment

Solomon wrote, "Heartache crushes the spirit. . . . A crushed spirit dries up the bones" (Prov. 15:13; 17:22). Grief—"a crushed spirit"—comes through many causes: a broken relationship; the loss of a loved one, a business, or a job; or broken dreams. It may come through a miscarriage or barrenness, or through disappointment in yourself or another person. We can even be disappointed by God, feeling that He let us down when we needed Him.

Victims of grief need to avoid the "If only . . ." treadmill of lamenting their own failure: "If only I'd made her stay at home, that drunk driver wouldn't have killed my daughter. She would be alive today." The enemy uses such tactics to produce guilt and despair, often leading to anger against God.

Grieving should follow a natural process over a reasonable time span. Counselors say this normally ranges from one to three years, although the process of healing may take longer for some. But unresolved, prolonged grief opens the door to spiritual, physical and emotional problems that paralyze spiritual growth.

A young mom at a retreat where I (Ruthanne) was once speaking came for prayer about her uncontrollable anger. "I overreact when my four-year-old daughter misbehaves—sometimes I even yell at her for no reason—and it frightens me," she said. Asking the Lord for guidance as to how to pray, I felt impressed to ask about her family background and her walk with the Lord.

She said her father had died suddenly when she was four years old. In an effort to shield her from grief, her mother and family members never told her how the death occurred, nor did they allow her to attend the funeral. Too bewildered to ask meaningful questions or fathom this loss at age four, she only knew her daddy never came home again.

Over the years she learned details of what happened, but her unresolved grief became a deep, bottled-up anger toward God for depriving her of a father in her childhood. When her own daughter reached age four, that anger began boiling to the surface in outbursts against her child and, sometimes, against her husband and even herself.

I assured her that God had not inflicted this tragedy upon her, but in our fallen world these things happen. Then I encouraged her to release her deep anger over this loss and to freely express to God the grief and anguish she had buried within herself for so long. As she poured out her heart to the Lord and began weeping, I comforted her as if she were that little girl crying for her daddy.

When her tears subsided, she looked up with a new brightness in her eyes. I urged her to continue opening her heart to the Lord during the remainder of the retreat, so He could heal her completely. She returned home feeling as if she had been freed from a bondage she hadn't even been able to identify.

In order to be free, the grief-stricken person must eventually be able to release her disappointment and say, "God, I don't understand this loss; but I choose to believe that You love me, and I put my trust in You." God can then pour out the "oil of gladness instead of mourning" (Isa. 61:3).

Addictions

Elizabeth goes to the beauty salon four times a week to maintain her impeccable appearance. Betty's addiction is sensual TV soap operas, while Faith's is the neighborhood spa. For Rhoda, keeping a meticulous house takes priority over her husband and children. Martha is a closet alcoholic, and Caroline is hooked on prescription drugs. All these women show signs of addictive behavior.

Webster's says that to be an "addict" means "to devote or surrender oneself to something . . . obsessively." The great danger of addiction is the matter of surrender—allowing the will to become passive. Most addicts insist, "I can stop any time I want to!" But until they become willing to submit to the power of the Holy Spirit to gain release, the chains hold them. Scripture warns, "Abstain from the sensual urges (the evil desires, the passions of the flesh, your lower nature) that wage war against the soul" (1 Pet. 2:11, *AMP*).

Caroline was in church every Sunday with her husband and two small children, seemingly a model wife and mother. But for 10 years she was addicted to prescription drugs and wine. She worked as a nurse and had no trouble getting doctors to write prescriptions for her—mainly for weight loss.

"Often when I popped a pill, I'd cry out, 'God, help me,'" she said. "But I couldn't control myself. I wasn't the mother I needed to be, but I liked the high the drugs gave me, and it was a good escape. I'd follow the pills with wine to help me feel calm."

One day her sister-in-law came for a visit and shared about how she talked to God. *I'd like to talk to God like that too,* Caroline thought. A few days later she met a missionary who challenged her to ask Jesus to truly become Lord of her life. Although she did ask the Lord to come into her heart, she continued popping pills and drinking. Later, she was shocked to read in the Bible that her body is the temple of the Holy Spirit (see 1 Cor. 3:16-17).

"Lord, if Your Spirit is in me and I am Your temple, I don't want to abuse something so sacred," she prayed. "Please help me stop taking these pills."

Determined to be set free from drugs, she searched the purses in her closet and got out all the pill bottles she'd stashed away. That night she flushed more than a thousand pills down the toilet, never to take another. And she suffered no withdrawal symptoms.

Three weeks later, while sipping wine one evening, she heard a voice say, "That will be the last drink, Caroline." She looked around and saw no one. Believing it was the Lord, she knew she had to chuck the wine too. She poured it all down the sink and never craved it again. God's power had broken her bondage!

Caroline has been free of drugs and alcohol for more than 30 years. Best of all, she has a close personal relationship with Jesus. Today she is a strong intercessor for her family, community and nation.

Addictions—whether to drugs, alcohol, self-gratification, pornography, perfectionism or negativism—usually stem from a desire to escape painful or difficult circumstances. But of course the addiction, which has spiritual roots as well as spiritual consequences, only deepens the problem. Christian psychologist Dr. Archibald Hart writes:

> All addictions have spiritual roots. Human nature is inherently rebellious and selfish. It desires self-aggrandizement and self-satisfaction. Addictions are a direct reflection and outcome of our life of bondage to this rebellion—traditionally called sin. No healing is complete . . . that does not address and remove this bondage. . . .
>
> There are many ways in which addictions can be spiritually destructive. . . . They are forms of spiritual idolatry; they sap energy and demand attention; they create a false barrier between the addict and God; they prevent obedience to God; they perpetuate sin.[1]

Often a person is driven to addictive behavior because of abuses in childhood, rape, rejection, a negative self-image, unforgiveness, guilt or grief. If addictive patterns are in the family line, that susceptibility should be taken into account and dealt with. Ask the Holy Spirit to show you the root cause of the addiction—either your own or of the person with whom you're praying—and seek healing and deliverance in that area.

Such bondage is not always broken instantaneously as Caroline's was. Breaking a bondage of addiction can be a long, hard road as addicts struggle to overcome their compulsions. Christian counseling and support groups are helpful to make the person accountable and provide encouragement. Victory comes by persevering in prayer, having a willingness to accept help from others and trusting in God's mercy. If we *will* to be free, we can break the bond of addiction by the power of the blood of Jesus, and then we can live and walk in the Spirit (see Gal. 5:16-26).

Rejection and Negative Self-Image

Words—ours or those of others—have the power to wound or to heal the spirit. One survey indicates that it takes at least five positive statements of affirmation to counteract the effects of one negative comment made to an individual. "The tongue that brings healing is a tree of life, but a deceitful tongue crushes the spirit. The tongue has the power of life and death" (Prov. 15:4; 18:21).

I (Quin) once prayed with an attractive woman in her forties who had the mistaken idea that she was fat and ugly. She had grown up in a rural area, and whenever her family had driven past a farm with pigs, her mother had teasingly said, "Look at all the little Deenas out there. Watch them eat!"

Wounded by her mother's words, Deena struggled with a "fat" image all her life. We revoked and broke that word curse during a time of spiritual warfare and prayer. Then we declared that she was God's workmanship created for His glory, and we thanked the Lord that Deena was created in His image. She was released from that bondage and is now able to see herself in a new light.

Rosa discovered the power of a word curse when Robert, her fifth-grader, came home with a low grade on his semester's work. The teacher had written that she was giving him this grade because he was capable of doing much better.

"When I prayed about it, the Lord reminded me of words spoken by my mother-in-law when Robert was six months old," Rosa told us. "She became angry with my husband when he asked her to not be so hard on her thirteen-year-old daughter. He hadn't asked her with the right attitude. Reacting angrily, his mother said, 'Wait till Robert's older. You'll find out what it's like not to be able to handle a kid in school!'"

Rosa recalled the Scripture: "No weapon forged against you will prevail, and you will refute every tongue that accuses you. This is the heritage of the servants of the LORD" (Isa. 54:17). Using that in her son's situation, she prayed and broke the words his grandmother had spoken over Robert so many years ago. His grades improved immediately, and soon he was chosen as one of two students in his class to appear on a television program because of his exceptional learning ability. To Rosa it was confirmation that the word curse was broken.

Illicit Sexual Activity

"Do you not know that he who unites himself with a prostitute is one with her in body? For it is said, 'The two will become one flesh.' . . . Flee from sexual immorality. . . . He who sins sexually sins against his own body" (1 Cor. 6:16,18).

Any sexual activity outside marriage—whether heterosexual, homosexual, child abuse, self-abuse, bestiality or whatever—is sinful, and God's people are continually warned against it. The current epidemic of sexually transmitted diseases bears out Paul's warning: "For the wages of sin is death, but the gift of God is eternal life in Christ Jesus our Lord" (Rom. 6:23). Where sexual sin is concerned, the wages can be physical, spiritual and/or emotional death. This type of sin also can open the door to demonic influences.

A victim of incest or rape, though she didn't willingly engage in the sexual activity, is nevertheless held by an invisible chain to her aggressor. Because this chain affects her relationship with God and with other people and affects her emotions and her self-image, we recommend intensive counseling in such cases—preferably with a Christian counselor specializing in sexual abuse. Such counseling provides the victim the opportunity to express her strong emotions and move toward forgiving the aggressor, so she can be truly free.[2]

A frequent result of sexual sin is abortion, which has serious spiritual consequences for the woman who makes this choice.[3] The testimony of an anonymous writer who underwent two abortions—the second one after having become a Christian—supports the claim of such consequences.

Following an abortion at age 20, a traditional churchgoer committed her life to Christ and began studying to become a missionary doctor. But while in medical school, she dated a backslidden Christian and became pregnant again. With no support from her boyfriend, and because of a drive to pursue her educational goals, she had a second abortion, which only compounded her problems.

"How ironic it all was," she wrote. "I was willing to lie, cheat, and kill in order to 'work for Jesus.' Next to my personal goals, my child's life was not important. Such a selfish agenda almost cost me my life and sanity."

She repented and received God's forgiveness, but because she could not forgive herself, the enemy oppressed her with thoughts of suicide.

"Satan oppresses women who choose abortion, bombarding them with guilt, condemnation, remorse, self-justification, self-loathing, and suicidal thoughts," she wrote. "These spirits come through the spiritual door the abortion has opened to the enemy—spirits from which the woman must be delivered. A spirit of murder directed inward had a stronghold in my life. I was so oppressed that I could actually hear the demons sing to me: 'Wanna die, wanna die, wanna die!' This went on for many weeks."

Her deliverance came when God spoke to her in church through this Scripture: "I will not die but live, and will proclaim what the LORD has done. The LORD has chastened me severely, but he has not given me over to death. Open for me the gates of righteousness; I will enter and give thanks to the LORD" (Ps. 118:17-19).

"I realized that I had a choice," she wrote. "I didn't have to die! I could live! Those suicidal thoughts were the devil talking to me. I went home preparing to do war. I pushed my front door open and spoke to the enemy as I walked in: 'This is it, Devil!' I studied Psalm 118 and Isaiah 38:18-19, and then forgave myself and the men in my life who had hurt me.

"It was completely dark in my bedroom, with no light coming in from the street as I got in bed. I remember praying, and then I saw three rust-colored beings appear on my ceiling. I told them: 'I'm going to live and not die, so I can declare the works of the Lord. The living will praise him. Death cannot praise the Lord; the grave cannot celebrate him. I'm going to live, and I'm not going to die! Get out, and don't ever come back again, in the name of Jesus.'"

When she repeated those last words, the evil beings disappeared.

"Because of God's mercy, I am still alive. The Lord has chastened me, but he has not given me over to death. Now I am completely free from that spirit of suicide, and I endeavor to live a life that honors the Lord."[4]

Occult Involvement

Deuteronomy 18:9-14 declares that occult activity is an abomination to God. Such activity includes astrology (reading horoscopes), palm reading, Ouija boards, Tarot cards, séances, fortune-telling, witchcraft, divination, sorcery, magic, casting spells or hexes, secret societies, and more.

An amazing number of Christians expose themselves to demonic influence by going to a fortune-teller and then laughing it off, saying, "Oh, but I didn't take it seriously." But the truth is, evil spirits *do* take it seriously. Others innocently purchase or accept as gifts objects that have occult significance. Such activity opens a door to the enemy, and God's Word speaks strongly against it.

Years ago, I (Quin) did a thorough housecleaning of such objects by going from room to room in my house and asking, "Lord Jesus, is there anything here connected with the occult or the demonic realm that is an abomination to You?" I got rid of face masks from the West Indies, Greek souvenirs with images of mythical goddesses, a world map bordered with astrological signs, an Indian painting and wall hangings that missionary friends told me had Hindu deities on them. I found some souvenir dishes given to me that had pictures of Roman gods painted on them. Out they went.

God's warning to the Israelites is as appropriate for us today as it was then: "The images of their gods you are to burn in the fire. Do not covet the silver and gold on them, and do not take it for yourselves, or you will be ensnared by it" (Deut. 7:25).

A friend of mine finally got free of depression after she and her prayer partner burned a stack of comic books that her husband had been collecting for eight years as a future investment. Satanic and New Age teachings filled their pages, and my friend had had no peace since he'd started bringing them home. "It took over an hour for them to burn—it was as if those books didn't want to be destroyed," she said. "But when they were gone, my depression lifted, and my husband was glad he'd agreed to let me burn them."

Consider these actions of Paul's converts in Ephesus: "Many of the believers who had been practicing black magic confessed their deeds and brought their incantation books and charms and burned them at a public bonfire. (Someone estimated the value of the books at $10,000)" (Acts 19:18-19, *TLB*).

Ask the Holy Spirit to reveal to you any literature or objects in your home that are dishonoring to God, and then destroy them and dedicate your home to the Lord.

Walking Free

The bondages described here frequently entangle God's children and render them powerless in spiritual warfare. If the devil cannot get you to renounce your faith altogether, he will try to ensnare you with these traps and make you ineffective. These are steps you can take in order to walk free:

1. Identify the problem; ask the Holy Spirit to show you any areas of bondage you may have overlooked.

2. Confess and repent before the Lord the sins the Holy Spirit reveals to you.

3. Choose to forgive all who have wounded you; also forgive yourself. Release your anger and disappointment toward God.

4. Receive the Lord's forgiveness and cleansing.

5. Renounce the sin and declare that all doors where the enemy has gained entry are closed and sealed by the blood of Jesus.

6. Ask the Holy Spirit to help you break the thought and behavior patterns you've become accustomed to (see Phil. 4:7-9).

7. Allow the Holy Spirit to daily conform you to the image of Christ.

Walking free from these bondages is important for your own spiritual wellbeing. But addressing these issues also will increase your effectiveness in fighting for your children, which we discuss in the next chapter.

Prayer

Father, thank You for shining the light of the Holy Spirit into my heart and revealing to me the areas of bondage where I need deliverance. I humble myself before You and confess my sins of rebellion: [name the areas of sin you wish to confess, speaking out what the Holy Spirit reveals].

*I renounce these sins and declare they will no longer
have dominion over me. I close all doors where the
enemy has gained entry, and I ask You to seal these areas
with the blood of Jesus. Holy Spirit, help me to focus
my thoughts on the things of God and break my negative
patterns of thinking and acting.*

*Father, I forgive [name] for wounding me; I release him
[or her] from all judgment and ask You to minister to his [or her]
deepest needs. I release my disappointment in You because this
happened, and I choose to obey Your Word, which says, "Get rid of
all bitterness, rage and anger, brawling and slander, along with
every form of malice" [Eph. 4:31].*

*Thank You, Lord, that I am cleansed and called to freedom,
not to slavery; and I will not be ensnared again with a yoke of
bondage [see Gal. 5:1,13]. I will walk in my freedom,
in the mighty name of Jesus. Amen.*

Fight for Your Children

Don't be afraid of them [your enemies]. Remember the Lord, who is great and awesome, and fight for . . . your sons and your daughters.

NEHEMIAH 4:14

All her clothing was black, except for a white turtleneck splashed with prints of skulls and crossbones. As she scooted past me to claim her middle seat on our flight to Vancouver, I (Ruthanne) was shocked to see that under her long hair, one side of her head had been shaved. Her silver jewelry depicted various witchcraft symbols. Pasty-looking makeup, heavy eyeliner and mascara, and dark red lipstick spoiled her youthful good looks.

She can't be more than sixteen, I thought to myself. *It looks as if she's caught up in the witchcraft fad I've read about ensnaring so many teenagers.*

Her chatter revealed that she was just a typical youngster going to Canada to visit relatives over spring break. "My mom's afraid I'll have trouble going through immigration," she said to the young man in the window seat, nervously brushing her hair to camouflage the shaved area.

Lord, she's so young and naive, with no idea of the danger she could be getting involved in, I began to pray silently. *Father, please reveal Your truth to her. Have someone who can get her attention witness to her. Give her mom wisdom to know how to deal with this situation.*

As almost any Christian parent or grandparent of preteens or teenagers would tell you, today's young people face pressures and temptations that were nonexistent when we were growing up. Clearly, the devil has targeted our children for destruction. Like a lioness protecting her cubs from predators, we women need to fight for our children.

A godly mother prays for each child from the moment she cradles her newborn in her arms—sometimes even when the child is still in her womb. And those prayers continue throughout her child's life. Like Jesus' mother, she ponders things in her heart (see Luke 2:19,51). At every stage of their development, a mother talks often to God about the children she has borne.

The Battle for Our Offspring

Though many parents seem unaware of it, a battle rages today on many fronts to win the allegiance of our children. Humanist-oriented educators for years have been propagating their philosophy through curricular programs in public schools. Initially aimed at neutralizing the basic Judeo-Christian view on which our nation was founded, these programs and their propagators now seek to eradicate these principles. Some years ago the late Mel Gabler, a textbook researcher, shared this insight:

The wording of many texts is designed to first sow seeds of doubt in the student's mind concerning his present values. Gradually he reaches the position of not believing anything; then the texts subtly indoctrinate the student with new "values," such as anti-Americanism, hatred for the home and family, man as an animal, and anti-Christian attitudes.[1]

Historian David Barton refers to these efforts as revisionism, which he defines as "the common method employed by those seeking to subvert American culture and society [by claiming] that the Founders 'reared a national government on a secular basis.'" Even a cursory review of the vast numbers of the Founders' original writings shows this claim to be false, yet the trend persists.[2]

An alarming number of curricular programs instruct teachers in how to introduce their students to such ideas as undermining authority figures; demeaning traditional family values; legitimizing witches, casting spells and other aspects of the occult; and affirming themes of despair, hopelessness, manipulation, violence and sexual experimentation. These ideas convey to impressionable youth the suggestion that each person can determine for himself or herself a customized worldview with no foundation in absolute truth.

We also see Satan's influence in the aggressive marketing of commercial toys, video games, cartoons, TV shows, movies, children's literature and secular music. Having been desensitized to the reality of evil in our society, some adolescents unknowingly are connecting with dangerous pedophiles on Internet social networking sites. It is a time for praying parents to be vigilant in cultivating godly values and a Christian worldview in their children.

New Age Versus the Power of God

The "do-it-yourself" sort of religion called New Age, which is a mixture of Western atheistic humanism and Eastern mysticism, is rapidly replacing our cherished Christian values. There is, however, nothing "new" about it at all. But it is very dangerous because its proponents have high on their list of objectives the indoctrination of our children and youth. Former occult practitioner Greg Reid writes:

In the last few decades, the New Age has come into full blossom and become part of much of our culture, media and education. If there is a common agenda, it is for One

World, one religion, global peace, and realizing man's Divinity. . . . It is tolerant of all faiths, except one—Biblical Christianity. One is free to believe anything one wishes, so long as one does not believe that the Bible is the only truth and the infallible, inspired Word of God and that Jesus is the only way to salvation. . . .

Some teacher, some movement or some spiritual activity may be 99% good—but if it contains 1% lie, you still become 100% deceived. . . . Satan is the father of lies, was a liar from the beginning and still lies, even if he puts on an evangelical suit or a clerical collar. Deception is his most potent weapon. It will be his final weapon.[3]

The risks facing children and youth today may seem too frightening to be real, but they are real indeed. And kids from Christian homes in our communities are not immune from these dangers. We as "watchmen on the wall" need to be aware of Satan's devices and withstand his work through prayer and spiritual warfare. We truly are at war with Satan, and the lives of our children are at stake.

"To fight well you must walk in the power of God," Reid says. "No more ignoring the forces of evil. I challenge you with the words of one teen Satanist girl: 'How do you expect me to believe your God has power over the devil if YOU don't believe it?' "[4]

"Power" is the key word here. Power is what occultism is all about, but we women of prayer have a greater power available to us.

The Danger of Rebellion

A primary problem many parents have today is their kids' rebellion against any form of authority. This is the sin that caused Satan to be cast out of heaven, and Adam and Eve to disobey God's instructions (see Isa. 14:12-15; Gen. 3:1-6). Scripture declares that "rebellion is like the sin of divination, and arrogance like the evil of idolatry" (1 Sam. 15:23a). Our heavenly Father knows the pain parents feel when their child rebels, only to suffer the inevitable consequences. Here's how one mom dealt with her son's rebellion.

"Excuse me, son," Hilda said, interrupting Jim, her 16-year-old son, as he shouted protests about his curfew hour while she cooked supper. Pointing her finger toward the angry teenager, she said, "Satan, you can't have my son. I bind your activity in him, in the name of Jesus Christ." The she calmly asked, "Now, Jim, what was that you were saying to me?"

"Oh, Mom, I just forgot," he said, turning to leave the room.

It was the first time Hilda had used her authority as a believer in Jesus to come against the devil's manipulation or manifestation in one of her children. Though all four of her kids had been reared in a Christian environment, all of them rebelled and chose their own path instead of God's.

About the time Jim's rebellion became a problem, Hilda discovered through her Bible study that the fight was not with her son but with demonic forces that bound him. From that point on, her prayers intensified with one goal before her: to see Jim, still living at home, as well as her older children turn to the Lord.

It was a long battle. Jim's rebellion persisted, leading him into drugs, crime and a stint in jail. But for years this determined mother persisted in prayer and warfare. Jim was released from jail, got a job and found a bride. However, like his siblings, he continued to go his own way.

One year when all four of her adult children and their spouses were visiting for Christmas, Hilda told them the only gift she wanted from them was one hour of their attention. She set up her Sunday School flannel board and took them on a Genesis-to-Revelation tour through the Bible, zeroing in on Christ's sacrifice on the cross for their sins. Captivated by her lesson, the group sat around the dining table for two more hours, asking Hilda questions.

The Holy Spirit began wooing them, and one by one over the next few months, they all committed their lives to the Lord. Today all of them have a vital relationship with Jesus. They look back on that Christmas roundtable discussion as a turning point in their lives.

"The enemy had ensnared all my children, and I knew I had to fight for every one of them," Hilda explained. "It wasn't an easy battle. But knowing it was not God's will for any of them to perish, I persisted in declaring to Satan that they are God's property, and he had to take his hands off them!"

A poll by The Barna Group reveals just how essential it is for parents to be responsible for their children's spiritual formation:

> Overall, less than four out of every ten young people (38%) said that churches have made a positive difference in their life. . . . Parents must take the lead in establishing the centrality of faith experiences and practices for their children. That begins with parents modeling the significance of faith in their lives. It also highlights the importance of families taking the lead in the spiritual development process, rather than expecting or waiting for a church to produce spiritual growth in adolescents.[5]

One mom dealing with a rebellious son said it well: "I've learned the importance of praying the Word of God over him instead of just 'praying the problem.' I'm confident that he will fulfill the destiny God has for him."[6]

Depression, Anger, Suicide

About the time Carrie's son, Matt, entered high school, he began having problems getting along with his father, who had grown up in a dysfunctional family. His father continually criticized Matt and seemed incapable of showing him any affection or approval.

"I was constantly praying Malachi 4:6—that the heart of the father would be turned to his son and vice versa—and asking God to heal their relationship," Carrie says. "My husband got into therapy, but because of his own problem, he had difficulty trying to make things right with Matt.

"One day as I was in prayer, the Lord said to me, 'Great fear is coming upon you, but you will have victory over it.' I didn't know what that meant, but I increased my prayer time, especially when the oppression in the house seemed so heavy."

That fall, as Matt began his senior year, he was depressed because he didn't like school, and he was upset that he didn't have a car of his own. Carrie was very troubled about his interest in a character in a horror film and was repelled by a poster Matt had put up in his room with an alien monster figure on it.

"More than once I went into his room and bound the evil spirits I felt he was allowing into his life because of this interest," she said. "When I confronted him about the creature on the poster, he just laughed and said, 'He's my friend!'"

Shortly after school started, a tenth-grade boy in the community committed suicide by driving his car off a cliff. As Matt's depression got worse, he once told his father he felt his mind was about to snap. Carrie and her husband prayed in agreement, pleading the blood of Jesus over Matt and asking God to protect their son from suicide.

One morning Carrie had a heart-to-heart talk with Matt about his depression and his girlfriend problems, and then she shared some Scriptures with him before he left for school. Through the day she prayed, "Lord, be a shield about him, be his glory and the lifter of his head" (see Ps. 3:3). She also asked God to raise up intercessors to pray for her son. Late that afternoon Carrie returned from a brief shopping errand just in time to see Matt as he was leaving for choir practice and Bible Study.

"God bless you, son," she said as he went out the door. "Have a good time, and I'll talk to you tonight." Carrie sensed that this pronouncement would somehow prove accurate—but not in the way she expected.

A few hours later Matt drove his mother's car off a three-hundred-foot cliff in the same area where the other boy had died, only higher up. Matt had said good-bye to his girlfriend and then he had driven to the cliff to read his Bible and pray, trying to reach God. Feeling there was no response, he started the car motor, rammed the accelerator and drove off the cliff.

As soon as the wheels left the road, Matt realized that he had made a mistake. He prayed, "Jesus, please forgive me. Take me home." Thinking he was going to die, he blacked out just before the car landed.

A woman living nearby saw what had happened and phoned the police as the car crashed on the rocky seashore below. Matt crawled from the wreckage in shock. Two Christian policemen walked up to him. "God must really love you, son, because He saved your life," one of them said. (These men had seen four or five other suicide attempts from that cliff; Matt is the only one who survived.)

The policemen saw a Coast Guard helicopter overhead and signaled for help. "Who called you?" one officer yelled over the noise as they lifted Matt into the chopper.

"No one—I just happened to be in the area," the pilot answered.

Within minutes Matt was in the trauma unit of a nearby hospital. When his parents arrived, he was conscious and able to talk. What Carrie had spoken over her son that afternoon came true. God did bless him by saving his life, and she spoke to him *alive* that night!

Matt came through the experience miraculously. He wore a brace for a few months because of a back injury, and he began therapy with a Christian psychiatrist. The doctor couldn't understand what had made Matt do this. When he said he had patients from families with many more problems who hadn't attempted anything so drastic, Carrie shared with him about the influence of the demonic realm.

In the emotional aftermath following the crash, Carrie cried out to God one day, "Oh, Lord, what was I doing at the exact moment of the crash?"

"That makes no difference," He replied. "What made a difference is what you were doing *before* the crash."

While Matt was in the hospital, Carrie ripped that horrible poster off his bedroom wall, and he never objected. Over the years since this crisis, Matt has reconciled with his father, made great progress spiritually and today is married with a family of his own.

What's a Mother to Do?

As a mother, you must be observant and aware of your children's activities and interests, and try to meet their friends. It is important to pray for your children to form godly friendships and also to pray for the friends themselves. Ask the Holy Spirit to show you specific areas you need to address in your prayers.

Counselors working with youngsters who struggle with suicidal tendencies or get involved with the occult suggest being alert to these indicators:

- extreme mood swings: black depression, violent rage
- nightmares and deep fears
- withdrawal from and rejection of family; noncommunication
- frequent absenteeism and lower grades in school
- interest in occult reading matter, unwholesome games and horror movies
- secret friends and reluctance to have you meet them
- compulsive lying and excessive swearing
- rebellion
- interest in heavy-metal music
- sexual promiscuity

If you suspect a child is now involved in or is being drawn toward any of these areas, naturally your first recourse is to pray. Pray for God's wisdom in handling the situation, and also pray that the child will have a revelation of truth and recognize the enemy's attempt to destroy him or her. It is helpful to pray in agreement with your husband or a prayer partner—don't carry the burden alone.

If you discover something questionable (such as a suicide note, occult objects or illegal drugs), ask the Lord to show you how and when to confront the child and whether you should immediately seek professional counseling. Timing is important. Don't jump to conclusions or become angry. Give the child an opportunity to explain, and accept what he or she says at face value. Ask the Lord to guide you to a competent Christian counselor and to reveal anything being hidden that should be addressed.

Fix on the Right Enemy

When 20-year-old Anna dropped out of church and began devoting all her time to Barbara, a girl she'd met in college, Valerie, her adoptive mother, went to war using the Word of God. After being deeply hurt by her boyfriend, Anna had lost interest in men altogether and had begun focusing on women's sports. Valerie tried to talk to her about the unhealthy relationship with Barbara, but Anna became defensive and belligerent.

This praying mom recognized that Barbara was not the enemy but only the means Satan was using to try to destroy Anna and keep her from fulfilling God's call on her life. So she searched her Bible and compiled Scripture-based prayers that she began praying for Anna daily. Some verses she paraphrased included these:

Even the captives of the most mighty and most terrible shall all be freed; for He will fight those who fight us, and He will save our child, Anna (see Isa. 49:25, *TLB*).

Thank You, Lord, that You have hedged up Anna's way with thorns. You have built a wall against her so that she cannot find her paths. She has followed after her lovers, but she shall not overtake them. Lord, You will betroth my daughter to You in stability and in faithfulness, and she will appreciate, give heed to and cherish the Lord (see Hos. 2:6-7,19-20, *AMP*).

The Sovereign Lord wakes her ear to listen like one being taught. She will not be rebellious, nor draw back from Him (see Isa. 50:4-5).

The Lord our God teaches Anna what is best for her; He directs her in the way she should go. She pays attention to His commands, her peace is like a river, her righteousness is like the waves of the sea (see Isa. 48:17-18).

The blood of Jesus purifies Anna from all sin, for He is the atoning sacrifice for her sins (see 1 John 1:7; 2:2).

Some years later, Anna finally opened up to share her struggles with her mom, admitting her rebellion and wrong attitudes, her need for healing and her desire to be reunited with her family. Finally she moved out of the city where so many evil influences pressed upon her, and she found a new job with a Christian boss. She slowly began replacing the negative elements in her life with positive ones as she renewed her commitment to the Lord.

"The battle for Anna was long and fierce, but the experience drew me even closer to my Commanding Officer," Valerie said. "Today my husband and I have a close, loving relationship with our daughter."

Pray for Your Children Groups

After reading Quin's book *How to Pray for Your Children* and watching the accompanying video, five women at a small retreat in Kentucky had the idea of forming groups to pray for one another's children.

Elizabeth, the leader, said, "Among the five of us we had about thirty children and grandchildren, and we saw the enemy was seeking to destroy them. We asked God to teach us how to pray and how to organize."

They began meeting weekly in local parks to pray for one another's children. About 20 women (sometimes husbands joined them) would meet for corporate prayer and to share testimonies of answered prayer. Then they would break up into small groups of four or five. Each person in the small group would share a specific need about one of her children or grandchildren; then the group prayed for that child. At the close of the session, each woman would take the name of one child (other than her own) to pray for throughout the coming week.

All needs shared in the small groups were held in confidence by the group members. Sometimes the leader would assign people to groups as she was led by the Holy Spirit, or they would simply count off to form the small groups. Week by week, parents had their faith boosted as they heard encouraging reports of how God was at work in answer to their prayers.

The original prayer group has since multiplied. Doors opened for them in various local churches to share the vision, and now, Pray for Your Children groups have spread throughout churches in the Lexington area as praying parents unite to pray for one another's children. Whenever I (Quin) am in Lexington, members of the original group meet with me for a glorious time of fellowship and prayer. Recently I learned that after the death of Elizabeth, their leader, they now meet only occasionally, but they continue to exchange prayer requests via phone. As their children's families grow, the prayer needs continue and the prayer coverage is intensified.

If you are waging a prayer battle for your son or daughter, be assured that God is working in the unseen realm to impact your child's life. As we've seen in the examples in this chapter, if you refuse to allow the enemy and discouraging circumstances to deter you, victory will come. Yes, your warfare prayers do make a difference. And it is always too soon to quit!

Now let's discuss various strategies that will help safeguard marriages against the enemy's attack.

Prayer

*Father God, Creator of all things, thank You for the gift
of my children. Please dispatch angels to watch over them and
protect them in all their ways [see Ps. 91:11], and send Christian
friends into their lives to help them and be a godly influence.
Lord, what an awesome privilege and responsibility to be a
parent! Give me wisdom to be the parent I need to be and
discernment to know when my children need my prayers or when
I need to be an understanding friend to them.*

*Father, may my children fulfill Your plan and purpose
for their lives. May "the Spirit of wisdom and of understanding,
the Spirit of counsel and of power, the Spirit of knowledge
and of the fear of the Lord" be upon them [Isa. 11:2].
I release these gifts You've given me, Lord, and place my
children in Your hands. Thank You that You love them more than
I do, that Your plans for them are plans for welfare and peace,
not for evil, and that You will give them a future of hope
[see Jer. 29:11, AMP]. Amen.*

Fight for Your Marriage

Wives, in the same way be submissive to your husbands so that, if any of them
do not believe the word, they may be won over without words by the behavior
of their wives, when they see the purity and reverence of your lives.

1 PETER 3:1-2

"My husband, a Bible-study leader, is physically attracted to a woman in our church fellowship. Please pray with me for him, Ruthanne," Alicia pleaded after hearing me teach at a Canadian conference.

"When this woman goes to Carl's office for spiritual counsel, he puts everything aside to spend time with her. Yesterday he did it again," she continued, beginning to cry. "He didn't even bother to call and let me know he'd be late coming home. Sometimes I get so angry, I just want to stop fighting for our marriage. He says he's not sexually involved with her, but he's playing with fire and doesn't even realize it. And he's an officer in the group sponsoring this conference!"

It's an all-too-familiar story of a Christian couple whose marriage is under attack. Because of his pride and his carnal nature, the husband enjoys the interest and attention of a woman seeking his advice, yet he's blind to the danger involved. The wife recognizes the peril, but feeling hurt and rejected, she directs her anger at her husband instead of at Satan, the real enemy. The rift gets wider, and unless prayer and sober counsel prevail, divorce can result.

Reports of infidelity in Christian marriages have sent shock waves through the body of Christ in recent years. What is the answer? Is the influence of our permissive society just too great for Christians to overcome? What can a wife do under these circumstances?

I told Alicia that I felt Satan was using this woman's attention as a snare to ruin her husband's testimony and his marriage. I advised her to renounce her hurt and anger and then forgive both of them.

Alicia prayed and forgave Carl and the woman involved. Then we bound the spirits of deception, pride and lust in both of them. We declared in the name of Jesus that all ties of sexual attraction between Carl and this woman, or any other women he had lusted after, were broken. We asked the Holy Spirit to reveal the truth to him, to expose the enemy's snare and to bring Carl to repentance.

"Now that you've released your husband from your judgment, the Holy Spirit is free to work in this situation," I told her. "Don't argue with him about it anymore. Just ask the Lord to help you express love to him."

I was astonished by the swift response to our prayer and spiritual warfare. After the meeting that same evening, I saw Alicia in the ladies' room, and she was radiant.

"Ruthanne, I can't believe the change in Carl" she exclaimed. "The Lord must have dealt with him during the service, because he came down from the platform during the offering and apologized to me for his involvement with that woman and for hurting me. I told him I forgave him. His whole attitude has changed, and I know the Lord will help us work everything out."

This is an example of approaching a marital problem through spiritual warfare. And in this case it appears that a much more serious problem was avoided.

A Wife Learns Mercy

In today's permissive society, pornography is a growing problem that threatens many Christian marriages. While Rachel's husband, Bob, was out of state for several months on a job assignment, she discovered that he had been making phone calls to pornographic 900 numbers and charging them on their credit cards. Rachel felt rejected, ugly and cheapened. She called Bob and confronted him with what she had found out, flying into an emotional rage as she talked. He cried and said he wanted to come home and talk it over and work things out, but Rachel refused. Then she called an attorney and scheduled an appointment.

"Only then did I settle down and ask the Lord what He wanted me to do," she said. "He showed me that taking my case to a lawyer was not the answer. Then He told me to begin praying for a spirit of understanding. I cancelled the appointment and said, 'God, You told me You would be my defense—I'm depending upon You.'"

About this time Rachel met one of Bob's aunts whom she'd not met before. From her she learned that Bob had suffered much rejection during his childhood. His mother had married five times while he was growing up, and he often went to this aunt's house to hide when he was afraid of being beaten by a stepfather.

Bob hadn't received affirmation or positive words as a child; now he was making these calls because he wanted to hear what he thought would boost his self-esteem. Rachel realized that if they did get back together, she would need to speak positive words of life to him.

"As I was still struggling with my own hurt and rejection, God gave me a graphic illustration of the blessing of mercy," she told us. "The year before I had opened a small business in my home, for which I filed sales tax receipts with the state each month. Now that the business had been dormant for six months, I assumed that I didn't need to send reports.

"One day a man from the state attorney's office came to my door and bluntly told me I could be prosecuted and sent to jail. Shaken, I explained that I simply was unaware that reports had to be filed if no sales were made, and my papers hadn't even been unpacked since our last move. Suddenly his gruff attitude changed. 'Well, I'll have mercy on you this time and take care of these reports for you,' he said.

"After he left, I stretched out on the sofa and cried. I was being bathed in mercy such as I had never experienced before, and I dropped off to sleep. When I woke up, I called Bob and told him I wanted to show him mercy. I was willing to talk things out."

The Lord gave Rachel Scriptures to pray for Bob: "Father, I pray that Bob will not set any vile thing before his eyes and that he will have nothing to do with evil [see Ps. 101:3-4]. Bob's body is not made for immorality but for the Lord [see 1 Cor. 6:13]. Thank You that he is free in Christ Jesus, and he will not be burdened again by a yoke of bondage [see Gal. 5:1]."

Many Scriptures also ministered to Rachel: "When anxiety was great within me, your consolation brought joy to my soul. . . . When I called, you answered me; you made me bold and stouthearted" (Ps. 94:19; 138:3).

When Bob came home, the couple met with their pastor for counseling. Bob repented, and Rachel asked him to forgive her for her bitter words.

"God not only set my husband free, but He also did a lot of changing in me, as He helped me to begin speaking encouragement and life to Bob," she reported. "For any woman facing this problem, I advise her to wait on the Lord before she takes any action. Then she should get counsel from a godly person and get her emotions under control before confronting her husband. We need to be willing to see the whole picture from God's point of view and work toward healing instead of rejection."

Love Can Be Tough

In one marriage poll, *100 percent* of the women interviewed said they considered faithfulness the most essential requirement for a spouse. Physical attraction was listed by only 19 percent of the women (ages

18 to 24) as being essential.[1] Clearly, a woman wants her husband to love her faithfully and exclusively all his days. Yet stark reality reveals that not all will.

Suppose your husband has had one affair after another and seems impervious to your efforts to get him to deal with the issue. What do you do?

"The lure of infidelity is an addiction to an individual who has a chink in his moral armor," says Dr. James Dobson, author of *Love Must Be Tough: New Hope for Families in Crisis.* In discussing the cases of three wives he'd interviewed who put up with infidelity in their husbands without confronting them, he says:

> While some people are chemically dependent on alcohol or heroin or cocaine, this kind of infidel is hooked on illicit sex. Psychologically, he needs the thrill of the chase, the clandestine meetings, the forbidden fruit, the flattery, the sexual conquest, the proof of manhood or womanhood, and in some cases, the discovery. . . .
>
> What they needed were wives who were committed to the concept that *love must be tough.* . . . What is required is a course of action—an ultimatum that demands a specific response and results in a consequence.[2]

A woman wrote Dr. Dobson telling of her experience after a counselor advised her to confront her adulterous husband, a pastor who had been dismissed from his church:

> The counselor told me not to take the blame for my husband's affair, and that nothing I had done could justify his infidelity. He advised me to stand up and be firm with him, even though it would be difficult.
>
> A few months later the crisis came. I gave Milan an ultimatum: either go with the other woman or stay with me. He could not have both of us any longer. I put my hands on

his shoulders and looked him straight in the eye and said, "You know you are to blame for what has happened to us. You committed adultery. I didn't." I told him if he loved the other woman more than me, then he should leave. I would accept it. I reminded him that he had a soul and would someday answer to God.

Milan not only broke off the affair, but he later thanked me for having the courage to stick it out with him through this difficult time. It was not easy, but we worked it out and our family survived.[3]

Seek God's Direction

A woman confronted with evidence that her husband is having an affair often reacts in one of two extreme ways.

The first is to ignore the evidence—or rationalize it—and go on with life as if nothing has changed. Some men are happy to continue living two lives, and their wives accommodate them. In fact, in many parts of the world, it is quite acceptable for a man to have a mistress on the side. And in some cultures a man is free to take a second wife and move her into the house. The first wife must either accept it or move out and support herself and her children. I (Ruthanne) have counseled and prayed with countless Christian women in Africa, Asia and Latin America who face these situations.

The other reaction is to confront the husband prematurely out of hurt and anger. This kind of confrontation usually ends in an emotional shouting match, where nothing is resolved, but the breach is widened.

The wise woman who suspects her husband is unfaithful should first of all go to her prayer closet and seek God's direction. Recognize that your husband is not the enemy, nor is the other woman. Satan is using the human weaknesses of all involved to try to destroy your marriage. Ask the Lord to uncover the things being hidden and to guide you step by step in addressing the issue. If you have a prayer partner who is truly able to keep confidences, you may consider asking her to pray with you for guidance and strategy.

Dr. Archibald Hart gives some further advice for a woman in this predicament:

> Divorce is not the only answer to an unhappy marriage. I am convinced that the solution to most miserable marriages is to be found in creative counseling, sound marriage guidance, and, if necessary, individual therapy for the marriage partners—as well as in a mutual turning to God for help and healing. . . .
>
> Of adults who are surveyed five years after their divorces, only about a quarter are resilient—managing to cope adequately with their new lives. Half are muddling along, just barely coping. And the final quarter are either failing to recover or looking back with intense longing to the time before their divorces, wishing the divorce had never taken place. Far from taking care of all their problems, for these people divorce has just added a whole set of new ones.[4]

Dealing with Abuse

Some years ago, Carmen shared with us her experience of enduring what she called a hellish marriage. Steve married her because she was pregnant with his child, but he would humiliate her without any regard for her feelings. After 10 years of frustration, Carmen got involved in an affair with a man she met at church.

"Of course I realized later how badly deceived I was," she said. "When I learned my lover's best friend was going to expose the affair, I decided to confess to Steve. When he asked why I'd done it, I told him it was because he never expressed love to me, and I was starving for someone to value me, to give me a sense of self-worth."

After repenting for her sin and making a new commitment to the Lord, Carmen asked God whether she could leave her unhappy marriage. God challenged her, "Are you willing to be made willing to love your husband unconditionally? And to treat him with as much love and kindness as you would Me, the Lord Jesus?"

Her answer was yes, she was willing to be loving and kind, even if she didn't receive love and kindness in return. But she felt the Lord would not require her to be treated like a doormat. So when Steve berated her, she simply replied firmly but kindly "Don't talk to me like that, Steve—your attack is unwarranted." After several such responses, her husband began to change. Once he came into the kitchen and said, "I'm sorry for what I said. Will you forgive me?" And of course she did.

When Carmen stopped lashing back at Steve's angry words, Steve saw that he couldn't get into a fight, and he would back down. By establishing boundaries, she earned his respect as she would embrace him and say, "This behavior really is beneath you— I know you're a loving, caring man." The Lord helped her respond to Steve's hurtful words with a right spirit, and over time, he became kinder in his treatment of her. Today they have a solid marriage and are enjoying their grandchildren together.

An abusive husband is obsessed with trying to control his wife's behavior by using emotional manipulation—accusations, blame shifting, anger, threats, tears or even silence—because he wants to feel as if he is in charge. Putting the focus on her behavior rather than on his own faults or weaknesses, he may falsely accuse her of the very sins in which he himself is involved. He tries to isolate her from family and friends and so intimidates her that she feels powerless to stop the mistreatment or find help.

When verbal and emotional abuse continues unchallenged, it often escalates to increasingly serious attacks of physical abuse. These episodes frequently are followed by apologies and promises that it will never happen again, but more often than not, it does happen again. Instead of simply clinging to the hope that this time he means it, a woman in such a relationship must refuse to be manipulated.

Yes, Scripture mandates that we forgive those who offend or betray us, but we strongly believe that a woman who is being verbally, emotionally or physically abused should take action to protect herself while fighting this spiritual battle. One minister advises the following:

1. Pray for the abuser. People who continually hurt others are in bondage to their own sin. And while that in no way excuses them, it gives you insight into how to pray for them. God intended these relationships for good, but they're undermined by alcohol, anger, and other counterfeits Satan uses to destroy fellowship and family. Pray for the abuser to become the person God intended.

2. Take a firm stand. You may need group support and a mediator present for an intervention. God's light can penetrate the deepest darkness with hope, restoration, and reconciliation, and when that happens it's a quicker path to healing. Nevertheless you need to take a firm stand, and if need be, get others to help you.

3. Ask God, "Should I stay or go?" It would be naïve to suggest that an intervention, sprinkled with prayer, will suddenly change everything. Some people respond to confrontation; some are melted by God's love. But many remain toxic and abusive, even when confronted in love, forgiven, and drenched in grace. You may need to end the relationship, as difficult as that may be. Remember, it's not your job to change the person, and it's not a failure on your part if they don't change. [5]

When a Marriage Fails

Unfortunately, some marriages do fail, no matter how much prayer or forgiveness is extended. God does not force obedience; a spouse might choose the wrong path, leaving the Christian wife or husband no recourse but to dissolve the marriage.

Dane assured Lonnie that he was a believer, but after the wedding she realized his deception. For 11 years she prayed for Dane's salvation. At times he went to church with her, but nothing in his life reflected a Christlike change.

After he retired from the military, they moved to the Middle East, where Dane worked for private industry and drew a huge salary. Consumed with greed, he stashed his money in Swiss bank accounts and invested in stocks and properties. These assets were placed in the names of various members of his family, but Lonnie found out much later that nothing was in her name.

While Dane's life was spinning out of control because of his alcoholism, Lonnie drew closer and closer to the Lord. Once after Dane had been on a six-day drunken binge, Lonnie heard what sounded like demons screaming through her husband, "Go in and kill her! Go in and kill her! Go in and kill her." She ran for her life.

Lonnie eventually went back home, but then Dane, who had been trained in psychological warfare, began using those tactics on Lonnie. He would tell lies about her, calling her a spiritualist, and he almost succeeded in turning her own parents and sons against her.

"I know God hates divorce, and I kept telling Dane I was committed to keeping our marriage together," she said, "but one day he filed divorce papers. Then I recognized that his heart was hardened, not only against me, but also against God. And he denied he had an alcohol problem."

Lonnie learned that God will not overwhelm the will of a person who refuses to yield his heart to the Lord. Neither could she argue her husband into the kingdom. The divorce was granted, with Lonnie receiving three years of alimony.

"The Lord has provided a meaningful life and ministry for me over the years since the divorce," she said. "I had stood on the Word and declared Dane's salvation for so long, it became like an idol to me. I had to totally relinquish him to the Lord, with the prayer that someday, maybe when he hits bottom, he will see his need for Jesus. In the meantime, I'm going on with God and trusting Him to meet my needs."

Even for a newly divorced Christian like Lonnie, God can provide peace and strength if the Christian looks to Him. But the newly divorced Christian is also advised to immediately seek counseling so that the mistakes divorced people commonly make can be avoided. According to Dr. Archibald Hart, these mistakes include:

- condemning themselves, which intensifies their unhappiness
- not dealing with guilt feelings in a constructive way
- changing things too quickly, making adjustment even more difficult for all concerned
- making promises they can't keep
- forcing the children involved to make painful choices
- acting without a sense of self-awareness[6]

Women Have Problems Too

It's not always the men who get caught in the adultery trap, of course. We hear reports of women who get involved with a co-worker or the boss at work, a trainer at the health spa, their pastor, their best friend's husband, or even someone they meet in an Internet chat room. Of course, most of these women don't plan to have an affair. But they don't take precautions against it, and they fall into the trap.

"Beware of letting a male become your confidante," warns one woman who had a five-year affair with her married boss. She was devastated when he announced that he was taking a job in another city and their relationship was finished. She turned to the Bible for comfort, recommitted her life to Christ and set about saving her own marriage.

In her book *Feelings Women Rarely Share*, Judy Reamer offers this analysis of sexual temptation for a woman:

When a woman is not being emotionally satisfied in her marriage, she often begins to fantasize what another lifestyle may be like. Even though she may have a satisfying physical relationship with her husband, she still may feel deprived in the area of intimacy. She may be married to the strong, silent type who does not communicate or listen to what she is trying to say. Or she may be married to a selfish or demanding man who is a taker rather than a giver. . . . When unmet needs are combined with daydreams and fantasies, women become extremely vulnerable for an affair. . . .

Whether your source of sexual temptation is an old boyfriend, a man on the job, or only someone you have had a dream about, the solution is still the same . . . stop the thoughts. Nip them in the bud . . . do not let your imagination run away with you. . . . Affairs start in the head before they get to the bed.[7]

Meditation on the Word of God—a weapon sharper than any two-edged sword—helps us get out and stay out of immoral relationships.

With the help of the Holy Spirit, a difficult marriage actually can become a laboratory in which God's love has the power to bring restoration. In the process, when both partners are willing to cooperate with God, undergo changes and grow stronger in their walk with the Lord, wholeness can take place. Reconciliation can begin even when only one partner takes the initiative.

Marriage problems have no easy answers. But it is possible to build God-honoring relationships on a foundation of sacrificial love and a willingness to receive God's help and healing.

In the next chapter, we'll look at ways to pray and battle during a health crisis.

Prayer for a Believing Husband

*Lord, thank You for the marriage partner You have blessed me
with. Help me to revere, honor and trust him; and to speak with
wisdom, but always with the law of kindness on my tongue. May
my husband love me as Christ loves the Church, and together
may we serve You. Give us a deeper understanding of Your Word
as we seek to live by its standards and seek Your direction for our
family. I pray that [name] will increase in wisdom and favor
with You and his working associates, and reach his full potential
as a man of God. Protect him from the fiery darts of the evil one.
Help him to be the father and grandfather You intended for him
to be, a godly influence and a blessing to all who know him*
[see Prov. 31:26; Eph. 1:17]. *Amen.*

Prayer for an Unbelieving Husband

*Lord, it grieves me that my husband is not serving You, but I know
You love him and desire to bring him to salvation. May he see Jesus
reflected in my life. Help me to see him with Your eyes and love
him with Your love. Lord, I pray You will send a godly man to
share the gospel with [name] in a way he can understand and
receive. In the name of Jesus, I bind all evil spirits that are keeping
my husband from knowing his heavenly Father. Grant him repentance leading to the knowledge of the truth that he may come to his
senses and escape from the snare of the devil, having been held
captive by him to do his will. Lord, open his eyes so that he can
turn from darkness to light and from the dominion of Satan to
Your kingdom, receiving forgiveness of sins. Thank You, Lord, for
working in his life until this prayer is answered* [see Acts 26:18;
Rom. 5:5; 2 Tim. 2:25-26, *NASB*].
In Jesus' name, amen.

Spiritual Healing and Warfare

He [Jesus] called his twelve disciples to him and gave them authority to drive out evil spirits and to heal every disease and sickness.

MATTHEW 10:1

Paula and Jim rejoiced when their granddaughter, Tiffany, was born. But three days later she had a seizure, and doctors told the family, "The right front side of her brain is destroyed." So these grandparents went into warfare mode to battle against the enemy's plan to kill or cripple Tiffany.

They immediately began a barrage of prayer using the Word of God. "Satan, you have no legal right to attack this baby—she is bone of my bone and flesh of my flesh," Jim would declare.

The Holy Spirit prompted him to pray about the blood supply to the baby's brain. "God, put a new blood supply to the part of Tiffany's brain that is damaged. Thank You for hearing me. Thank You for doing it. New blood supply to her brain, Lord, new blood supply. Thank You, Lord."

Some time later, when they felt God's peace and a sense of release, they stopped their warring. Soon a nurse came to tell Jim and Paula that the baby had stopped having seizures. When Jim asked what time the seizures had stopped, he learned it was the exact moment he had sensed it was time to stop battling.

Four days later Tiffany went home from the hospital and never had another symptom. When her parents took her for her six-month check-up, the doctors said new blood had gone to the part of her brain that had been damaged, just as Jim had prayed. She never had another seizure and tested above normal in her development.

Paula and Jim have covered her with prayer throughout her life and look forward to attending her graduation from the University of Alabama when she finishes her studies.

Healing: Not a Formula

Just as there is no formula for spiritual warfare, Scripture does not provide a one-two-three formula for healing. Sometimes healing comes through casting out demonic spirits, sometimes by the faith of the person who is ill, sometimes by a prayer of agreement—but always by Jesus' sovereign supernatural touch. Three such outstanding healings that Jesus performed in Galilee are recorded in the fifth chapter of Mark.

The first involved a man tormented by evil spirits. He lived among the tombs and had such supernatural strength that no chains could hold him. Then he encountered Jesus and fell at His feet. Jesus commanded the evil spirits to come out of him and go into a herd of pigs. Immediately the man was restored to his right mind.

Next is the account of a woman who had been bleeding for twelve years but had not been able to be helped by doctors. Pressing through the crowds around Jesus, she reached out and touched His cloak. Immediately her bleeding stopped. Jesus told her, "Daughter, your faith has healed you. Go in peace and be freed from your suffering" (Mark 5:34).

The third healing concerned Jairus's young daughter. While on the way to Jairus's house to heal his daughter, Jesus heard that the child was dead. But Jesus said, "Do not be afraid; only believe" (Mark 5:36, *NKJV*). With her mother and father and his own disciples, Jesus entered the room where the child was lying. Taking her by the hand, He commanded, "Little girl, I say to you, get up" (Mark 5:41). The twelve-year-old stood up, walked around and then ate a meal. Not just healed, but brought back to life.

God's power to heal certainly has not diminished today. Sometimes He uses doctors and modern medical technology, as well as prayer and spiritual warfare, to bring about healing. I (Ruthanne) once interviewed a surgeon who used to be outraged when he saw ministers praying for the sick.

"I felt they were infringing on my territory," he said. "I figured they should stick to preaching and let me and my professional colleagues in medicine take care of the sick. But then I became aware of the work of the Holy Spirit. When a Kathryn Kuhlman meeting came to our city, they invited me to sit on the platform. I watched as a woman who was bent over, crippled by disease and in constant pain, was healed before my eyes. I could hear her bones snap as she stood up straight and began to walk freely, praising God. After that I began praying for my patients, and realized I needed God's partnership in trying to help them."

Another respected Christian doctor gives this perspective on divine healing:

With God there is no universal, cookie-cutter, one-size-fits-all approach to healing. Just as no two people on earth have identical fingerprints, no two individuals will have exactly the same pathway to healing! . . .

God may use traditional medicine, a mineral, a plant, an herb. He may use something as commonplace as the vitamins and chemicals in certain foods, or something as dramatic as a surgical procedure. . . . For me, the key is praying and being open to the revelation and leading of the Holy Spirit.[1]

Enemy Interference

God's best is for us to walk in divine health, although many complex factors—some of them our fault, some of them the work of the enemy—frustrate God's highest plan for our lives. But one thing is clear in Scripture: The devil's intent always is "to steal and kill and destroy" (John 10:10).

In every situation we face where spiritual warfare is called for, we need God's direction for wisdom and discernment. Here are brief accounts of three friends who shared the strategies God gave them as they stood in faith for their healing:

- Before seeing a doctor about her persistent headaches and dizziness, Judy and her husband went away to fast and pray for three days to seek God's wisdom and direction. She agreed to have surgery to remove a large brain tumor but knew she had to put her trust in God for complete recovery. Judy believes those days of fasting and seeking God prepared her for this battle. After eight weeks of recuperation, she left on a missions trip and never returned to her secular job. She has been involved in ministry ever since.

- Esther had had surgery four times to remove a growth under her arm that kept growing back. The doctor said if it came back again, it probably would become cancerous. She had been praying for healing, but when the growth returned a fifth time, Esther determined to trust God instead of returning to the doctor. Then she dreamed about a group of people standing around a coffin and saw herself lying there. In the dream she began rebuking and binding Satan, declaring he could not take her life. Next, she saw an evil figure on the flatcar of a train being quickly taken away. She woke up, certain she was healed; and when she felt for the tumor under her arm, it was gone.

· Peggy was almost killed when a hit-and-run driver sent her flying through the air against her car's windshield and then onto the street. She heard a bystander praying for her, and in the ambulance she and her husband prayed the Lord's Prayer together. Doctors stitched up the severed arteries in her leg but said she would need surgery the next day because she had a skull fracture and internal bleeding. The next morning, when her pastor came to pray and give her holy communion, she felt the power of the Holy Spirit as she took the sacraments. She knew she was healed. The doctor ordered new tests and soon returned to tell her the bleeding had stopped and surgery was not necessary. Peggy had a full recovery.

Battle of the Mind

Scripture indicates that the mind is indeed a battlefield, so it is important for an effective spiritual warrior to learn how to stand against the enemy in this area.

When Arlene Strackbein learned she was in the final, hopeless stages of multiple sclerosis, she had a dream one night in which she saw an open grave.[2] She knew the grave was hers, and fear squeezed her into the darkness. Then she heard a voice say, "Don't look down. Look up!" She awoke mystified and asked the Lord what the dream meant.

In her spirit she heard His reply: "Arlene, don't focus on the circumstances. Don't look at your problem. Look at Me. Look at My resources. Look at My love. Don't look down. Look up!"

Arlene learned the futility of calling détente with Satan. "We can't say to him, 'You leave me alone and I'll leave you alone,'" she said. "When we don't see a way out, our hearts falter and we find ourselves right where the devil wants us. He sucks us into the mire of helplessness and a no-win situation."

After the Lord gave her that dream, Arlene began to believe God to do the impossible as she resisted the oppression of the enemy against her mind and as she declared the truth of God's Word. Just as Nehemiah saw victory by refusing to go to the Plain of Ono to talk with the enemy who was taunting him (see Neh. 6:2-3), Arlene experienced victory as she followed the Lord's instructions to her. She filled her thoughts with Scripture and resisted Satan's tormenting thoughts. Some time later when she attended a healing service, she instantly was made whole.

Here is the principle God taught her that night about His divine perspective. Notice the contrast.

In the Spirit	In the Natural
Seated in heavenly places	In the plain of "Oh no!"
Alert and active	Drowsy and inactive
Beholding Him	Focusing on our problem
Moving in divine revelation	Listening to Satan's mockery
Receiving the kingdom	Calling détente
Confident of victory	Defeated

"No matter how defeated you may have felt in the past, no matter how your mind has been assailed by the enemy, change your mind to agree with God's best. Recognize that 'we have the mind of Christ' [1 Cor. 2:16], and look up to see His triumph."

Smith Wigglesworth had a remarkable ministry of healing in the last century, primarily because of his absolute faith in God's Word. He wrote:

Believers are strong only as the Word of God abides in them. The Word of God is spirit and life to those who receive it in simple faith. . . . Know your Book, live it, believe it, and obey it. Hide God's Word in your heart. It will save your soul, quicken your body, and illumine your mind. . . . Inactivity of faith is a robber which steals blessing. Increase comes by action, by using what we have and what we know.[3]

A Believer's Authority

When her daughter, Cathy, suddenly started having grand mal seizures, Gloria Phillips entered a new level of spiritual warfare for her child's healing.[4] (Gloria's own healing story appears in chapter 5.) As she began binding the demonic convulsive spirit (based on Matthew 16:19), Cathy's seizures diminished, but she still was experiencing convulsions.

Five specialists who originally treated Cathy could find no reason for the problem and labeled the convulsions idiopathic. Someone had to sleep with her because the convulsions occurred within 30 minutes of sleep and doctors cautioned her parents never to let her bathe without an attendant, swim, climb trees, ride a bicycle or drive a car when she was old enough.

Gloria fasted for weeks at a time, laid hands on Cathy nightly and prayed two hours every morning, claiming her child would be healed. Although her faith was sagging and she felt there was nothing left to do, she prayed and asked God to send an angel. That is when real breakthrough began to come, but Gloria shared this fact with no one except her husband.

Much later, one night after Cathy had had a convulsion, an angel did come and touched her with the sweeping of his wing. "I know I am healed," she told her mom the next morning, and she dumped her meds into the garbage disposal. After more than four years of seizures, she never had another.

Today, 40 years later, Cathy is thoroughly healed. She became a sales rep for a major pharmaceutical company and drove constantly, covering her territory with a perfect driving record.

Several years after Cathy's last convulsion, Gloria learned more about the spiritual dynamics of what they had experienced. She heard a tape of an evangelist telling about praying for a convulsive child in England. The child's mother told him a man dressed in black and wearing a black opera cape had been seen on the property where they were living.

"Who killed themselves here?" the evangelist asked. "Take me to where it happened."

The mother took him to the spot where the former owner of the property had committed suicide. When the evangelist commanded the demonic spirit controlling the situation to leave, through the power of Jesus' name, the child was instantly set free.

Suddenly, Gloria remembered that shortly before Cathy's first convulsion, Gloria's mother had had a similar experience in the home where they had lived at the time. She had seen the image of a man dressed in a black opera cape appear in the hallway and then instantly vanish. Gloria felt the similarity of these instances was too remarkable to ignore.

The original owner of the Phillips's former house had committed suicide near the area where Cathy and her older sister slept. The family who lived in that house after the Phillipses moved away had a young son who slept in the same room. He developed muscular dystrophy and died. When Gloria's family had held meetings in the den, in the vicinity of the area where the suicide had occurred, the Holy Spirit was hindered. But after moving the group to the front of the house, the meetings were free and attendance increased. Those who attended had commented on that fact.

The next time Gloria and her husband visited that city, they went to their former house, laid hands on the outside walls and bound the spirit that had consistently tormented all the families who had lived there. "We cleansed the property spiritually for the present occupants and any future owner," Gloria said. "No other child who has lived there since has had any difficulty."

Choose Life!

Fran is a woman of faith who learned a new depth of spiritual warfare when her husband needed emergency heart surgery. Mike had been in a wheelchair for 35 years as a result of polio. He was now a 67-year-old triplegic with heart complications. Though doctors said his chances of survival were minimal, they air-evacuated him to a large-city medical center for surgery.

A prayer partner called to give Fran this verse to encourage Mike: "When I passed by you and saw you squirming in your blood, I said to you while you were in your blood, 'Live!'" (Ezek. 16:6, *NASB*).

"Mike, do you want to live?" she asked her husband the night before surgery. "I don't want you to be praying to die, while I'm praying for you to live. I want to honor what you want, because things could get rough in this battle."

"I want to live, Fran," he assured her. "I feel God has some things left for me to do. I love life, so of course I want to live."

Holding his hand, Fran prayed aloud, "Lord, we now agree and declare *Mike chooses life*. If we hit any tight places in the days ahead, we are in agreement with Your word to Mike that he does choose life. Thank You, Lord."

The surgery went smoothly, and when doctors felt all was under control, they allowed Mike to make the six-hour trip back to his home. But the first night home, Mike began to hemorrhage. He was rushed to the local hospital and his condition stabilized with transfusions, but over the next 40 days, he literally fought for his life. Doctors pumped 15 units of blood into him.

One night after Mike was moved to a private room, he began hemorrhaging again. Fran quickly called for help and a medical team hurried to get IVs going in his arms, legs and chest. He had no detectable blood pressure and his vascular system was collapsing. Fran, a nurse, knew he was dying.

While the medical team was working, she knelt down and looked Mike in the eye. Though he couldn't respond, she knew he could hear her.

"Mike, choose life," she shouted. "Choose life, Mike. Choose life . . . choose life . . . choose life. You will not die but live. Choose life." Fran watched Mike's eyes until she was sure he understood. Even though he couldn't breathe on his own, she knew that both fight and light had come back into him.

During his long hospital stay, prayer warriors gathered outside his room day and night to join Fran in fighting for his life. They'd pray, saying Bible verses aloud and declaring to the devil that he wasn't going to snuff out Mike's life prematurely. He would live.

And live he did! For the next 20 years Mike had an active life in his wheelchair, and God used him and Fran to teach and mentor many people in their home.

Praying Around the Clock

Many committed intercessors were involved in fighting for Mike's life, and his story confirms that to have a group of spiritual warriors praying in agreement, standing on God's Word, is a powerful strategy. Jody's story is similar.

Having been born with a kidney disease, most of Jody's young life had been plagued with illness. By the time he was eight years old, treatment with a dialysis machine was no longer effective, and at that point, Jody received a kidney transplant from his father.

All went well until the third day, when the transplanted kidney suddenly stopped functioning. The doctor told Sharon, Jody's mother, that the kidney would have to be removed the next day.

"No, wait. I have a church family who prays," she begged.

Sharon called Barbara, the pastor's wife, who immediately called two other prayer warriors to join her in prayer. That night at the midweek service, volunteers signed up to take one-hour shifts around the clock to pray that Jody's body would not reject the new kidney.

"We are to pray until he comes home from the hospital," Barbara instructed the volunteers. "No letting up. Jody's life depends on this prayer, so please do not sign up unless you intend to keep your commitment."

Prayer warriors filled all the time slots and went to battle. Within 24 hours, the kidney began functioning properly, but the prayer support team kept praying until Jody left the hospital. Amazingly, he was able to go home on the day originally scheduled for his dismissal.

Later, when Barbara visited him at home, Jody told her that whenever he was in a lot of pain at the hospital, there was something like a dark cloud that would hover over his bed. But when his mother or grandmother prayed, it would disappear through the wall. When they stopped praying, that "something" returned to hover over his bed, and he would again have extreme pain. The prayers literally drove away the spirits of death, pain and oppression that had tried to take the child's life.

Today, because of intercessors who were faithful in prayer to battle for the boy's life, Jody's transplanted kidney is functioning normally.

When Healing Doesn't Come

While the examples of healing we've shared are primarily victories, sometimes healing doesn't come. Most of us have family members or friends who we prayed would be healed, but they did not recover. We don't have answers as to why this happens, but it is only realistic to acknowledge that the time will come when we all die. However, it is also realistic to acknowledge that as we trust God to allow us to live out our days on the earth to do His will, sometimes a spiritual battle will be required.

From our study of the Bible, we continue to believe that it is our business to pray and God's business to heal, in His way and in His timing. He still gives His followers authority to drive out evil spirits and heal sickness, in His mighty name. Let's not stop!

Intercessors often ask us, "How can I recognize when I am under attack?" In the next chapter, we will explore this topic.

Prayer

Father, I give You thanks for the promise of Scripture declaring that Jesus bore our sins on the cross, and by His stripes we are healed [see 1 Pet. 2:24]. I choose to believe Your Word, and I put my trust in You for healing for [name]. Lord, if there is pride, unforgiveness, disobedience or unbelief obstructing the flow of Your healing power, please reveal it; and give grace for repentance and correction. Strengthen my faith as I fill my mind with Scripture and wait upon You for direction and strategy. Father, I choose to keep my focus upon You and to find joy in each day You give. Thank You, in Jesus' name, amen.

12

How Can I Tell
If I'm Under Attack?

*Beloved, do not think it strange concerning the fiery trial which is to
try you, as though some strange thing happened to you; but rejoice to the
extent that you partake of Christ's sufferings.*

1 PETER 4:12-13, *NKJV*

By now you have discovered that just because you are a Christian,
you are not immune to the attacks of the evil one. But you have a
direct line to the One who can free and heal. How do you know if
you are under attack? How can you discern whether evil forces are
at work in your life or if it's God at work?

One teacher suggests that you ask yourself, *Is what I'm experiencing a temptation, a test or an attack?*

- If it's a *temptation*, I want to resist! I could choose to say as
  Joseph did when tempted by Potiphar's wife, "How then
  could I do such a wicked thing and sin against God?"
  (Gen. 39:9).

- If it's a *test* sent by the Lord to teach me something, I want to learn.

- But if it's an *attack from Satan*, I want to fight to see his plan defeated.

Does God test us and teach us? Yes. We read of His dealings with Israel: "These are the nations the LORD left to test all those Israelites who had not experienced any of the wars in Canaan (he did this only to teach warfare to the descendants of the Israelites who had not had previous battle experience)" (Judg. 3:1-2).

God wanted the younger Israelites to learn war through hands-on experience. We need to ask God what it is He wants us to learn in the situation we're going through and how to overcome any difficulty, and then we need to trust Him to show us what He wants us to learn or do.

What Is This, Lord?

JoAnne, an intercessor for a major Christian ministry, awoke one morning feeling as if she'd been kicked in the head by a horse. In moments, she was partially paralyzed. Rousing her sleeping husband, a military doctor, she told him, "You'd better get me to the hospital; I can't move!"

While waiting for the ambulance, JoAnne began praying, "Lord, are You about to take me home? If You are, I'm ready. But if this is an attack from Satan, I need to know, so I can fight. Which is it?"

"An attack!" She felt she'd clearly heard God's word.

"Lord, I know what to do with an attack—fight. And I'll fight for all I'm worth because that means You have something greater in mind for me. Now, please strengthen me to fight."

Stand. I'm in this with you, the Lord seemed to assure her.

During the next few days in the hospital, whenever she'd feel another swift "kick in the head," she would declare, "Satan, you've come far enough. You can't kill me. I'm hidden in Jesus. By His stripes I am healed. Now back off!" Then she'd sing and worship God for a long time.

Although doctors ran numerous tests and even sent her to an out-of-state hospital, they never definitely diagnosed her illness. The only abnormality the doctors found was a smaller-than-normal artery in her head, possibly a condition she'd had since birth. One doctor told her plainly, "I do not know what is wrong." Finally the paralysis and excruciating headaches left her, and she went back to her usual routine.

But whenever JoAnne feels another swift blow to her head, she knows it's an attack from Satan. She says, "Devil, and every demon spirit coming against my body to give me this infirmity, I tell you to stop your maneuvers in the name of my Savior, Jesus Christ. You are a defeated foe, and I am redeemed by the blood of Jesus." She continues to walk in victory today, and she mentors other women in warfare and intercession.

Am I Doing Something Wrong?

Once I (Ruthanne) was teaching on spiritual warfare for a women's group in East Texas. Afterward a woman shared that in her two-year walk with the Lord, she had led several family members to accept the Lord—she was one of the first in the clan to become a Christian. But now she was troubled about many serious problems she and her family were facing.

"Am I doing something wrong?" she asked.

"No, it's not that you're doing anything wrong," I assured her. "Your praying and witnessing have made you a prime target for the enemy because you're invading his territory. Actually, you should be encouraged to know you are a threat to the devil's kingdom. Take up your weapons and fight!"

Helping her with guidelines and Scriptures to go along with the lesson I had just taught, I prayed with her and encouraged her to find a prayer partner to stand with her in warfare concerning her family problems.

Her question—"Am I doing something wrong?"—is a question all of us ask at one time or another. How do we tell whether we're off track somewhere, or under enemy attack? Is the enemy opposing us, or is God trying to tell us something?

I asked some seasoned, godly women for wisdom in this area. "When the enemy attacks, there is great condemnation and seemingly no way out," a pastor's wife told me. "I distinguish by recognizing the difference between condemnation and conviction. Condemnation brings hopelessness. When the Holy Spirit convicts, there is a way out. I can confess my sin—of gossip, lying or whatever—and receive forgiveness and cleansing."

"The enemy will try to defeat us in some area or even remove us from the spiritual race entirely," another friend said. "God's correction, on the other hand, exposes a heart condition or weakness in some area. His correction gets us a better place in the race and keeps us in focus for the next battle."

"I have contested and rebelled against God's roadblocks," a young graduate student told me. "But I knew that I was acting in defiance of God rather than against the crippling influence of evil. Attacks by evil forces generally have been accompanied by a spiritual prompting for prayer against the opposition."

The following contrasts the characteristics of these two types of trial:

Enemy Attack	*God's Correction*
Accusation, condemnation of you	Conviction concerning the attitude or deed
Depression	Call to repentance
Hopelessness	Assurance of forgiveness
Destruction of self-esteem	Restoration of a sense of value as God's child

How the Enemy Gains Access

We asked more than 100 intercessors, "What makes a believer vulnerable to the enemy's attack?" They mentioned these major ways we can give the enemy access to our hearts, minds and bodies:

- sin (immoral behavior, disobedience, anger, pride, rebellion, unforgiveness, criticism, selfishness, and so on)
- ignorance of Satan's devices and characteristics
- compromise with the enemy
- limited knowledge of God's Word and His purposes
- not spending time with the Lord (lack of discipline and vigilance; becoming careless or passive)
- lack of persistence or focus in discerning between the voices we hear
- failure to use spiritual weapons (due to the above reasons)
- taking our eyes off Jesus and focusing instead on our problems
- immaturity (blind spots or areas of our life not yielded to the lordship of Jesus)
- fatigue (physical, emotional or spiritual)
- preoccupation with self and physical comfort
- inadequate prayer coverage by others
- disunity or contention with fellow Christians and in the home

Repeated Attacks

Sometimes, however, there seems to be no chink in your armor, no disobedience to God, no willful sinning, when *pow*, here comes an arrow aimed at putting you out of existence. Rowena felt like that when a drunk driver hit her car, causing serious injuries. God showed her that the accident was definitely an arrow from the bow of the enemy.

Since the Bible says that "no weapon forged against you will prevail" (Isa. 54:17), Rowena claimed that verse as she began her long convalescence. She also meditated on Psalm 23:4: "Though I walk through the valley of the shadow of death, I will fear no evil." When doctors said she might never walk again, she clung to that Scripture and used it in warfare. And she did walk again.

Five years later she had another car wreck. She was able to get out of the car and run to safety, just before her car rolled over an embankment and was totaled.

"This time a righteous indignation arose in me," she said. "I found that once again I had to put a guard on my mind by quoting Scriptures to resist fear that my life might be totally destroyed. Only a renewed mind can rise up in times of attack and defeat the purposes of the enemy."

Over the years, we have prayed with women who seem to have a pattern of repeated attacks of a certain kind within their families—divorce, addictions, car accidents, falls or other mishaps, miscarriages or abortions, occult activity, etc. In many cases this is because of generational bondages that need to be addressed. If you become aware of repeated problems in these areas, ask the Lord for direction and strategy to deal with them. (See chapter 8 for more details regarding this issue.)

Satan's Counterfeits

As our society becomes more and more materialistic, cynical about absolute authority, and charitable toward false religions, people are fooled into believing they can "be like God." This concept is the basic belief of New Age philosophy. But just as a frog doesn't jump out of slowly heated water and ends up cooked to death, so it is with one who dabbles in Satan's counterfeits. Destruction is certain unless the Christian sees the danger and gets out. Helen's experience reveals just how easily one can get caught up in deception.

Led by a lust for adventure, Helen rejected her orthodox Jewish upbringing and "innocently" began reading astrology columns. Soon she acquired her own personal astrologist to give detailed guidance for most of her life's decisions. Then she got involved in a sect of Hinduism.

"I had declared God dead but was quite open-minded about the occult," she reported. "My friends were dabbling in black magic and witchcraft, and though I was not officially involved, I was tolerant of those who were. I even had a Jungian psychiatrist who practiced divination by using the Chinese *I Ching*. I would acknowledge any god except the true God."

In the course of her spiritual wanderings, Helen's congenital lung disorder worsened, and she ended up being hospitalized with severe allergies 2,000 miles from home. Christians at the hospital shared the love of Jesus with her; then a Christian couple opened their home to her while she received outpatient treatment. The wife had an allergy problem similar to Helen's, but during her nine-month stay in that home, Helen saw her hostess, praying and trusting in Scripture, healed of her allergy problems. Helen herself had to return to the hospital, more desperate than ever.

"I needed confirmation that this Jesus thing was real, but I needed it from a non-Christian source," Helen said. "My Jewish friend, Anne, who also was into Hindu philosophies, came to tell me of a dream she'd had in which she was crying out for God to heal me. But He told her I would have to ask for myself. Although this was the end of February, she brought me an unusual token—a Christmas card that presented the whole story of Jesus Christ. 'Two months ago you weren't ready for this, but now you are,' she said."

Helen's defenses broke when she realized that God had used an unbelieving Jew—now a Hindu—to bring her the message of Jesus. It was a turning point. She allowed a Bible-study leader to pray for her healing, and she finally acknowledged Jesus as her Messiah. Immediately she was healed of several maladies, and the serious lung problem began improving.

"The person who led me to the Lord took me through the process of forgiving everyone I had any grievance against and renouncing the occult," she said. "Three weeks after accepting Jesus, I was baptized in the Holy Spirit; then I learned that my occultic past had attracted curses and demons. A minister prayed with me for three hours until the bondage was broken and a new freedom began. I had not studied Hebrew, but could recognize it from having heard it spoken as I grew up attending synagogue. My first prayer language was Hebrew—and that convinced me that I didn't have to stop being a Jew to be a believer in Jesus."

Helen destroyed books and objects that were blatantly occultic, and she continued the cleansing of her apartment as the Holy Spirit revealed other things to her she needed to get rid of. Over the following years she became one of my (Ruthanne's) prayer partners, and she also grew into a powerful spiritual warrior who helped others to sharpen their discernment. God used her mightily to minister deliverance to those who had been caught in the web of Satan's counterfeits.

Whose Voice Is That?

Women have often shared with us experiences of hearing a voice and wondering whether it was from God or not. Actually, there are three possibilities:

1. It could be God speaking through the Holy Spirit. If so, whatever is spoken will be consistent with God's character and His Word.
2. It could be a demonic voice representing Satan.
3. It could be your own inner voice "speaking" a thought based on your logical reasoning, your will and human desire, or your self-centered emotions.

If you have difficulty discerning which it might be, we suggest this warfare prayer:

Lord, I desire to hear Your voice and be led by You. If this is Your Holy Spirit speaking, please cause this impression I have to become clearer and more urgent. If You want me to take any action, cause the urge to do this thing to increase. If this impression I have is not of You, please cause it to fade. By the authority of the blood of Jesus that covers me, I command any evil spirits present to be silent, in Jesus' name, and to flee. I silence the voice of my own reasoning, desires and feelings. I refuse to hear any alien voice; I will listen only to the voice of my Shepherd. Thank You, Father, for speaking to me by whatever means You choose as I wait upon You. I promise to obey that which You speak. Amen.

The Enemy's Voice

When the hospital nurse brought Ruby's newborn to her for the first time, she was repulsed by the sight of her four-and-a-half pound preemie. He looked like an ugly, shriveled-up, 90-year-old man. In her mind she heard a voice say, "Throw him on the floor. You don't want him. Throw him on the floor."

"I hugged him to my bosom and withdrew into a corner of the room as though to protect us both," Ruby recalled. "Since I had lost three babies through miscarriages, I had bargained with God for this baby, as Hannah did for her son, Samuel. Naming him Michael, for the warrior angel, I promised God he would be a mighty warrior for Him."

Ruby recognized that an enemy voice had told her to destroy her baby, and she refused to heed the order. "It was as real as any voice I've ever heard," she said. "I know God gives life; He doesn't destroy. So I had no trouble knowing this was not God but an attack from Satan himself, and I ordered him to leave."

Most of us know that the enemy's voice is not always as clearly discernable as it was in Ruby's case. So it is important that we spiritual warriors fill our minds with the Word of God and remain vigilant and aware of the enemy's devices.

Instilling Fear

One of the enemy's primary devices is fear, and he uses various ways to instill it in a person. One young newlywed shared how she became aware of the enemy's attempt to instill fear in her and how she learned to resist this attack.

"I was a new bride living in an unfamiliar city, and my husband traveled extensively. Satan used my loneliness as a means of instilling fear, subjecting me to a series of noises. For several months, whenever my husband was out of town, I'd be awakened in the night by the sound of my husband's voice and noises he would make while working in his office. I could hear drawers opening and closing and the computer clicking. Although I was wide awake, the sounds would continue for some time and in great detail. I was greatly troubled by it.

"After several months of such occurrences, I was led by the Lord to come directly against the devil's schemes in the name of Jesus Christ. As I did this repeatedly, the noises stopped and never recurred. I received a great deal of strength and confidence, and my fear was replaced by well-directed anger at the devil. I learned that persistent prayer renders Satan powerless, and his attack cannot continue."

These stories illustrate how critically important it is that we learn to discern between God's dealings *with* us and the devil's attack *against* us. The next time you feel as if a ton of bricks has fallen on your head, you may want to ask, "God, is this a temptation, a test or an attack?" We desire to resist temptation, pass God's tests and to fight any satanic attack.

Remember, every time you win a victory, you are strengthened and trained for the next battle, and God will open opportunities for you to help liberate other believers under attack. Yes, a woman's place is in the war!

In our closing chapter, we share some valuable lessons learned by other spiritual warriors that will encourage and instruct you.

Prayer

Father, just as Jesus prayed that You would protect His disciples from the evil one, I ask that You also protect me and my loved ones. Teach us to clearly hear Your voice, see Your plan and follow Your direction. Teach us how to discern when we are under attack by the devil and how to use our weapons effectively. We love You, Lord, and our greatest desire is to serve You and to please You and to help set the captives free. Speak to our hearts, Lord, for Your servants are listening. In Jesus' name, amen.

Lessons from the Field

*No weapon that is formed against you shall prosper, and every tongue that
shall rise against you in judgment you shall show to be in the wrong. This
[peace, righteousness, security, triumph over opposition] is the heritage of the
servants of the Lord [those in whom the ideal Servant of the Lord is repro-
duced]; this is the righteousness or the vindication which they obtain from
Me [this is that which I impart to them as their justification], says the Lord.*

Isaiah 54:17, *AMP*

Women identify with those dealing with problems that are unique
to women. The following stories—lessons from the field—are actual
experiences of godly women who have faced problems like some of
you are facing now or may confront in the future.

In the Workplace

Both single and married women juggle work with family and other
interests to contribute their share to the household. Finding a job—
much less the right job—isn't always easy either. But as Eunice
learned, even when the job doesn't seem right at first, it may be exactly where God wants you.

With her children all enrolled in school, Eunice decided to return to her nursing career. She asked the Lord for a job where she could pray with patients who might be ready to receive Him. If she accepted the job she wanted, on the cancer floor of the university hospital, her bosses would be the chief of the oncology unit and the head nurse. The two were having an affair, and both were known to be anti-Christian. Eunice wondered whether she should take this job, knowing it would involve tests and trials.

At her interview, Eunice asked the doctor point-blank, "Can I pray with patients?"

"Aw, go ahead," he snarled. "I need you here immediately, so you're hired."

As Eunice went on her nursing rounds, she prayed for any patient who wanted prayer. But working with a doctor and head nurse who mocked her God was a challenge. She often overheard them swearing and making fun of her for actually believing that prayer could help anybody on a cancer ward. She didn't argue with them; she just called on the Lord for strength to keep at it.

One day when Eunice felt she'd been targeted for abuse, she heard the Lord whisper, "Don't let Satan remove you from where I've placed you and called you to stand." So she determined to keep praying and not to give up.

A year later the chief of the department and his head nurse were fired. Gradually, many other godless people were removed. Most were replaced by believers, and soon it was not unusual for several nurses to meet with Eunice in the supply room, their "prayer closet." They began talking openly to the patients about their Christian faith and have seen many come to know the Lord.

"It was anything but easy those first months," Eunice said. "The enemy wanted me to throw in the towel, but God wanted someone who could bring His life to the patients. I'm glad He helped me stick it out."

Fighting for Financial Breakthrough

With financial systems so unstable throughout the world, it seems that whenever my friends and I (Quin) meet for prayer, the cry is, "Lord, we need a financial breakthrough. We trust You to supply our needs. Come to our rescue."

The downsizing and merging of companies have contributed to widespread job layoffs, which in turn has led to an increase in the number of houses in foreclosure and bankruptcies being declared. Obviously, there is a need for God's intervention. In my small Florida community alone, more than 4,000 families were faced with losing their homes due to foreclosure in mid-2009.

Two friends who had buyers for their houses had removed their furniture in anticipation of moving. But just before closing on their house, they learned the potential buyers did not qualify for a mortgage, so they moved mattresses back into the empty houses and slept on the floor, praying and battling during the delay.

When another friend, Linda, and her husband moved to a smaller house, their larger one stood vacant almost nine months because the housing market had hit bottom following two hurricanes. I knew they tithed their income and were a family dedicated to the Lord, so I joined her in praying that the house would sell as we stood on God's promises to meet their needs. One day while praying with her, the Lord dropped into my thoughts something entirely different from what I would have imagined.

"Let's pray for the family who needs that house, can afford it and will enjoy it immensely," I said to Linda. "We'll pray the new owners will have as much happiness there as you did while raising your family in that place."

So we prayed in agreement a blessing prayer over the future owners. I also suggested that Linda go back to her property and pray on-site. Less than a week later I got an excited call. The roomy, two-story house had sold to a family with several children who needed to live near the military base. They loved the house because it was ideal for them. Relieved that the financial burden was lifted, Linda and her husband called their friends to share their "Hallelujahs" for answered prayer.[1]

Unfortunately, many families, out of work for months, have not had their financial needs met that soon. There also are a lot of people who have lost not only income from their job but also most of their investment and retirement funds, the latter wiped out when the bottom fell out of the stock market. Many retirees I know are struggling to stretch their income to meet their bills, especially medical expenses.

After a relative of ours sold their house and moved temporarily into a motel while the dad searched anxiously for a new job, their little girl remarked, "Mom, we don't have a home to go home to."

One prayer warrior whose husband lost his job told me (Quin), "I have learned I need to get a different strategy for every situation we face. Praying for finances and breaking the spirit of poverty or the enemy's hold are not the same. To break poverty, we made sure we tithed. We did everything we knew to fulfill the Word and stay in covenant with God so that Satan has no legal right to harass us. We also speak to the seed we've sown, asking God to restore what the enemy has stolen. What we lost shall be recovered."

She continued by pointing out the biblical example of David at Ziklag, when the enemy came in his absence, burned the city and took everyone captive. David was so discouraged, he wept and cried out to God. Then he strengthened himself in the Lord and asked God what to do. The Lord responded, "Pursue, for you shall surely overtake them and without fail recover all" (1 Sam. 30:8b, *NKJV*). David and his men pursued the enemy, fought, won and recaptured everything that had been taken. He not only brought back the spoils, but he also had enough to give to other cities.

"Remember, he recovered all and had spoils left to share," she concluded. "God wants to do that for us too. And I believe He will give us the needed warfare strategies to see victory."

Praying with Compassion

A praying mom whose son is living in the gay world says her situation has caused her to look at homosexuals in a completely different light: as a challenge for prayer and warfare. "My heart has been broken for my son, but I also weep for other young people—many from Christian homes—who are trapped in Satan's cruel deception," she wrote.

"I can't see a gay person on the street or in a store without thinking, *I wonder if anyone is praying for him?* One time an acquaintance, who doesn't know about my son, commented about a homosexual working at the hair salon she goes to. 'I don't want him to even touch me,' she said with a shudder. I can't imagine Jesus ever making such a remark. Suppose the woman caught in adultery [see John 8:3] had been a male prostitute? Would Jesus have encouraged the crowd to stone the man?

"I used to be incensed about the gay activists I read about in the newspaper. Then the Lord told me to start praying for them, as well as their families. I learned that the former president of the gay activist group in our city was the son of a Pentecostal pastor, and the leader who succeeded him was the son of an evangelical pastor. Both young men have since died of AIDS. As I prayed for them, God replaced my disdain with compassion for them and their families. How can we hope to win them if we treat them like lepers?"

In praying for our nation and the subcultures within it that so desperately need to see Jesus as He truly is, we must walk in compassion. John Dawson reminds us:

As you stand in the gap for your city, allow the Holy Spirit to shine the bright light of truth into the inner rooms of your soul. Run from the religious deceit that would seduce you into believing that you are superior to any person. It is only by the blood of the Lamb and the power of the Spirit that we stand free from the chains of guilt and the sentence of death.[2]

A Widow Overcomes Grief

The enemy often tries to use grief to paralyze a woman's emotions and nullify her Christian witness. If ever there was a woman who could have given in to her deep sorrow, it was Emily.

Emily was 27 when her test-pilot husband was killed. Crushed with grief, she blamed God for leaving her a widow with a four-year-old. Her mother told her, "Emily, Jesus is a Good Shepherd, and you are one of His little lambs. He will take care of you. Just trust Him."

Emily's anger toward God lifted as she began to study the Word of God and discovered that the Shepherd really did love her. She returned to college and then began designing children's clothes. Six years later she met a lawyer who proposed marriage.

"I knew I didn't love him like my first love, but by now I had grown in the Lord and could love him with God's love, so I married him. He was a kind, gentle man. But after we'd had sixteen years together, he died of a heart condition. Again I found myself a widow."

The Lord gave her this verse that helped her through her second bout of grief: "No one who puts his hand to the plow and looks back is fit for service in the kingdom of God" (Luke 9:62).

Emily has been a widow now for many years, and God has been a faithful husband to her as she presses closer and closer to Him. "I don't look back, because if I did, I would not accomplish what God has for me to do for Him today," she says. What she does for Him is head up the intercessory group at her large urban church.

Her advice for other widows:

- Don't let bitterness, anger or grief rob you of a fulfilled life today. Release those feelings to God.
- Thank God for the spouse you had and for the good years you enjoyed together. Be grateful.
- Trust the Lord to meet your needs in the areas where you once depended on a husband.
- Read the Word of God, study it, and get to know the Lord personally.

• Reach out to others, especially to other widows, and help bring healing into their lives.

Praying with Discernment

Janet's six-year-old son, Kevin, came in from school one day with a defiant, sassy attitude. "What did you do in school today, son?" Janet asked, puzzled by his mood.

"Played with a crystal ball the teacher brought. We asked it all kinds of questions," he answered.

"Lord, what shall I do about this?" Janet, a new Christian, prayed silently. From deep within she heard, "Break the witchcraft and curses that come with it."

"Kevin, come sit on my lap for a minute," she said, still asking the Lord *how* to follow the direction she'd just received. She gave Kevin a big hug as he climbed on her lap. Then she heard herself saying, "Father, in the name of Jesus I break the power of witchcraft and curses, and I take back from the enemy the ground he has stolen from my son. We give that ground back to You, Lord. Thank You for Your protection and Your blessing upon Kevin."

After prayer, Kevin immediately changed back to her happy, sweet-natured kid. "That was my introduction to dealing with invisible evil forces," Janet said. "In a nutshell, I quickly learned about spiritual warfare, and I'm still using it for both of my children."

When Kevin grew older, he began driving a huge cattle transport trailer-truck across the country. One night Janet woke up four times, and each time she "saw" a truck going off the road. The truck was the 18-wheeler Kevin was driving.

"I began binding the spirits of death and calamity, and then I asked the Lord to send angels to keep my son's truck on the road. I did it four times that night," she remembers.

At dawn Kevin called to say, "Mom, I'm back in town, but I'm too tired to drive home. Four times last night my truck almost went off the road. Were you praying?"

We need to be alert, sensitive to the Holy Spirit's nudging day and night, and available to do warfare and pray at a moment's notice.

Compromising Vows

Sometimes women open themselves to oppression from the enemy when they take an oath as part of an initiation in a secret society. During Rae's first weeks at college, she was thrilled when a social club invited her to join. Against the advice of her pastor and parents, she accepted, paid her dues and made a pledge. But the more she attended the meetings and participated in the group's activities, the more frequent her headaches and depression became.

In prayer one day, she asked the Lord to show her the root cause. "You took vows inconsistent with your Christian faith" was the answer she heard.

Rae repented, asked God's forgiveness and tried to get out of her commitment, only to be told she couldn't do it. She then called the national headquarters and demanded that her name be removed from the membership list, and she cancelled her vows.

"I was set free from guilt, depression and headaches—I knew I should never have joined that organization in the first place," she reported.

Others in similar circumstances may need to get rid of a ring or pin that symbolizes their vows, or renounce in prayer their association with any secret organization that compromises their commitment to Christ.

A Spirit of Bitterness

Any difficulty we or a family member faces in life gives us an opportunity to seek God's battle plan for resolving it. Ginger was more than concerned because her daughter Chris, a dedicated Christian, was in conflict with her college roommate. The girls had been close friends in high school and had looked forward to rooming together, but now arguments and disagreements were too common.

One weekend when Ginger stayed overnight in the dorm with Chris while the roommate was away, she discovered two disturbing facts. First, the previous year a violent race riot had exploded in that very dorm room, leaving some students with bloody noses. Second, Chris's roommate had made a cross-stitched plaque and hung it over their door: "Dorm Bitter Dorm"—a takeoff on "Home Sweet Home."

"It seemed the room had been invaded with spirits of anger, hate, rage, resentment and murder—spirits that had been 'invited' through rioting the previous semester," Ginger said. "And the sign above the door didn't help matters; it was like putting out a welcome mat for a spirit of bitterness.

"Chris and I removed the sign; then using Jesus' name and authority, we commanded the unclean spirits to leave that room," she told us. "Chris asked the Lord to forgive her for her part in the strife with her roommate, and we asked God to fill the room with His peace. The results were almost immediate. It seemed the air had been cleansed and a blanket of peace pervaded the room. The girls are no longer roommates, but they remain friends."

A Spirit of Lust

While Ginger saw a cross-stitched plaque inviting a spirit of bitterness into a place, another friend had to confront a spirit of lust.

While traveling on a ministry trip, Katherine was a guest in the home of a woman she had never met. As she put her suitcase in the guest-room closet, she was bombarded with lustful thoughts and feelings. She rebuked the thoughts and commanded that any evil spirits leave the room. Then she called her husband and asked him to pray for her. The thoughts left.

That evening when she opened the closet to hang up her clothes, once again lustful thoughts invaded her mind. She pulled the string to turn on the light and let go of it so suddenly that it flipped onto the top shelf of the closet. Reaching up to retrieve it, Katherine found a couple of magazines on the top shelf. She pulled them down and was shocked to see that they were blatantly pornographic.

Now she understood why a spirit of lust had attacked her mind when she had opened the closet. When she asked her hostess to come see what she'd discovered, the hostess told Katherine that she too had experienced lustful feelings whenever she cleaned that closet. The woman confronted her 19-year-old son, and he admitted this was his secret hiding place for his porn magazines. With the matter exposed, he agreed to counseling.

"Since then," Katherine said, "whenever I stay in a hotel or guest room, I make it a habit to command every unclean spirit that might be present to leave in the name and authority of Jesus Christ. All kinds of spirits dwell in hotel rooms where illicit sex, drug dealing, perversion and porn movies have been going on."

Once when I (Quin) checked in for a conference, the registration packet included the suggestion that each woman, once she got into her hotel room, declare aloud: "In Jesus' name, I renounce any claim to this room by Satan, based on activities of past occupants. I command all evil spirits to leave this place and never return." This is the recommended prayer that followed:

Heavenly Father, thank You for this room where we can fellowship and rest during our conference. I ask You to make this room a place of physical and spiritual safety for me and anyone else who enters it. I ask You, Lord God, to station holy, warring angels to set a guard around this room. Your Holy Spirit is welcome here. Send Him to bless us, even as we sleep in this place. Thank You, in Jesus' name, amen.

Providing Prayer Cover

People who travel in ministry quickly become keenly aware of their need for prayer coverage as they work on the front lines of confrontation with the enemy. A young woman missionary, after her first term of service in Southeast Asia, wrote in her newsletter:

> If folks at home don't pray for me, then I'd better stay at home! My reaction to my first term of service is that the mission field is like a fierce battlefield, in which there are no ceasefires. In an ordinary war, ground soldiers are not expected to fight unless sufficient air cover is provided; otherwise they might soon be wiped out.
>
> Constant overhead protection and reinforcements are vital. Any country sending troops into ground battle without such support might justly be accused of condemning these men to defeat and death.
>
> Similarly, it seems to me to be equally irresponsible for a church to send someone out as its representative into the warfare of the mission field, if that church is unable or unwilling to maintain sufficient, continual praying forces to defeat the enemy attacks that strike missionaries continually.[3]

Besides the importance of praying for missionaries, the need for prayer coverage applies in many situations: a husband or family member serving in the military or traveling and working in dangerous surroundings, a child at camp or college or living in a crime-ridden city, a Christian teacher trying to uphold godly standards in a public school classroom—the list goes on.

Are You Enlisted?

There are a lot of problems and challenges facing women today. And there is a great need for women of faith to join the ranks and pray for victory—in their personal life, their family, their neighborhood, their community, their nation and their world. Where are the Deborahs and Esthers of our generation?

The Deborahs are those who will get God's instructions and go to war against the enemy, confident that God goes before them to secure victory.

The Esthers are those who will intercede before the King on behalf of their people, those born for such a time as this, who will pay the price to get a wicked proclamation reversed.

Our liberation began with Jesus' death, burial and resurrection. Satan has no legal power over us, although he continues to wreak havoc in the world. Our Savior, the seed of the woman, crushed his head and broke his power. Now it's up to us to exert the authority Jesus invested in us to take back the ground the enemy has stolen.

We are authorized by Jesus and empowered by the Holy Spirit to do battle. With our orders from God's Word, we Christian women must take our positions in God's army. Let's learn how to pray more effectively and how to fight in the spiritual realm until those we love are truly liberated in Jesus.

"He Who lives in [us] is greater [mightier] than he who is in the world" (1 John 4:4, *AMP*). Therefore, we have nothing to fear! May the women who proclaim the good news become a great, invincible army!

APPENDIX 1

Arsenal Scriptures for Spiritual Warfare

For Authority over the Enemy
Isaiah 44:25-26a; 54:17; 55:11; 59:19
Jeremiah 1:12
Matthew 10:8; 12:28-29; 16:19
Mark 3:27; 6:7; 16:17
Luke 10:19
2 Corinthians 2:14
Ephesians 1:19-22; 4:8; 6:10-18
Colossians 2:15
Revelation 1:18

For Children
1 Kings 4:29
Psalms 127:3-5; 144:12
Isaiah 11:2; 43:5; 49:25; 54:13; 59:21
Jeremiah 29:11-14; 31:16-17
Daniel 1:9,20
Ephesians 1:17; 6:4
Philippians 4:19
Colossians 1:9-12
James 1:2

For Dealing with an Abusive Husband
Leviticus 26:3-13
Deuteronomy 8:7-10
2 Chronicles 15:7
Psalms 31:20-21; 32:7; 91; 144:11; 145:18
Ezekiel 28:24-26

For Guidance
Psalms 34:19; 37:23-24; 123:1-2
Proverbs 3:5-6
Isaiah 30:21
2 Corinthians 5:7

For Healing
Exodus 15:26
Psalm 103:3
Proverbs 3:7-8; 4:20-22
Isaiah 53:5
Matthew 4:23; 9:28-29; 15:26-28
Luke 9:11
1 Peter 2:24
1 John 3:8
3 John 2

For the Nations
Joshua 1:3
Psalms 2:8; 68:32-35; 108:1-5
Jeremiah 1:10; 15:19-21; 51:21
Daniel 12:3
Micah 4:13

For a New Job
Deuteronomy 28:3-14; 31:8
Joshua 1:3,5-9
2 Chronicles 15:7
Psalm 1:3

For Peace of Mind
Deuteronomy 33:27
Psalm 31:24
Isaiah 26:3
John 14:27
1 Corinthians 2:16b
2 Corinthians 10:5
Ephesians 2:14-15
Philippians 4:7-9

For Provision and Finances
Deuteronomy 8:18
1 Kings 17:2-4,8-9

2 Chronicles 32:8
Proverbs: 3:2; 10:3; 11:23,25; 12:12;
13:21-22,25
Isaiah 54:5
Malachi 3:10-11
Matthew 6:25,32
Luke 6:38

For Protection
Deuteronomy 28:6-7
Psalms 5:11; 17:7-9; 91:1-7,10
Proverbs 2:8
Isaiah 54:17

For Restoration and Security
Psalms 31:8; 32:7
Proverbs 10:30; 12:3,21; 18:10
Joel 2:18-32

For Sleeplessness
Job 11:18-19
Psalms 4:8; 127:2
Proverbs 3:24
Matthew 11:28-30
Mark 4:37-39

For Strength and Declaration of Victory
1 Samuel 17:45
2 Samuel 22:33,35,40
2 Kings 6:16-17

Psalms 18:29; 68:28; 149:6-9
Song of Solomon 6:10
Isaiah 41:15; 50:7
Jeremiah 12:5; 23:29

For Those in Authority
Psalm 37:23
Proverbs 21:1
1 Timothy 2:1-2

For Wayward Family Members
Psalm 140:1-2,4,8
Isaiah 59:1
Jeremiah 33:26
2 Corinthians 4:3-4
2 Timothy 2:25b,26

For Weariness and Depression
Psalms 28:7-9; 30:11-12; 55:18
Isaiah 40:28-31; 41:10; 43:2,18-19;
45:2-3

To Receive Jesus as Lord
John 3:7-8,16; 6:37; 10:10b; 14:6
Romans 3:23; 10:9-13
1 John 1:9

Why Pray
Ezekiel 22:30
1 Timothy 2:1-2
James 5:16

APPENDIX 2

Prayers and Declarations Based on Scripture

Oppose Satanic Interference
In the name and authority of Jesus Christ of Nazareth, I oppose any satanic tactics or strategies that are designed to hinder or delay God's plans and purposes from manifesting in their correct time and season in my family's life. [See Dan. 7:25.]

Authority over the Enemy—for Children
In the name and under the authority of Jesus Christ, my Lord, I bind all principalities, powers and spiritual forces of evil in the heavenly realm exerting influence over my child[ren], [name(s)]. Your assignments against them are cancelled by the blood of Jesus Christ.

I bind and break spirits of witchcraft, occult activity, satanic interest, mind control, fantasy, lust, perversion, rebellion, rejection, suicide, anger, hatred, resentment, bitterness, unforgiveness, pride, deception, unbelief, fear, sensuality, greed, addictions, compulsive behavior, and [add others the Lord reveals]. I break their power and the power of rock music, and I declare them null and void in the lives of my children. The blinders the enemy has put on my children must go, in Jesus' name. My children will see the light of the gospel of Christ; they shall be taught of the Lord, and great will be their peace [see Isa. 54:13].

I release them to be all God created them to be!

Break Curses
I declare that any curse that has ever been spoken against me and/or my family—any negative, evil word that has ever come against us—is broken

right now, in the name and authority of Jesus Christ of Nazareth. No weapon formed against us shall prosper.

Declaration

I declare that everything I put my hands to do is going to succeed and prosper. When the enemy shall come in, like a flood, God's spirit lifts up a standard against him [see Isa. 59:16-19]. "With God we will gain the victory, and he will trample down the enemies" [Ps. 60:12].

False Religion

Father, shield and deliver our nation from occultism, New Age deception, false religions and secret societies. Reverse the trends of humanism and socialism in our society.

Family with Division

We cry out for mercy today for our family, Lord. When the enemy comes in to divide, confuse, bring disunity, anger or hurt, Father God, intervene and be our Healer and Deliverer. Strengthen and restore our family. In Jesus' name, amen.

Family—Daily

Lord, I ask for You to bestow upon me and my family Your presence, provision and protection, and for Your precious promises to be fulfilled in our lives. I thank You that we are victors, not victims. You are fighting our battles for us. We have the favor of God.

Favor

"For surely O LORD, you bless the righteous; you surround them with your favor as with a shield" [Ps. 5:12]. I thank You for doing this for me and my family.

Finances

Lord, I war for the enemy to release finances and all resources that You want me to have for completing the great work You have given me to accomplish here on earth. I call in the resources necessary for me to do God's will to come without delay. Father, I thank You in advance for the wisdom and discernment I need to accomplish that task and to use those resources wisely.

Financial Lack

When financial setbacks attempt to lure us into fear, Lord, may we stand firm on Your promises. We declare that all our needs are met according to God's glorious riches in Christ Jesus. [See Phil. 4:19.]

Elections

Father, we pray that moral, God-fearing men and women be elected and supported in local, state and national elections. We pray for You to reveal Your choices, expose corruption, immorality, bribery, hidden agendas and special interests. May any unrighteousness that needs uncovering be brought to light and exposed. Let Christians be responsible voters and use the Bible as their plumb line.

Enemy Attacks

I bind every tactic of the enemy. Get off, get out, get away from our family's finances. You will not steal nor withhold from us what is rightfully ours through Christ.

Marriages

Lord, help our nation to return the state of marriage to a place of honor and establish this sacred institution in Your divine order. For marriages that are strained, bring hope and healing and restoration. Let Your Holy Spirit direct those couples who are facing critical decisions. Guard our families from strife and division, and invade these homes with joy, peace and comfort.

Nation

Father, we place our nation, cities and families under the blood of Jesus. We seek Your face, Lord, and repent of our sins—we are truly sorry for the way we have broken Your laws and disobeyed You. Thank You for forgiving us. Please heal our land. We declare that no weapon formed against our nation shall prosper. Every tongue that would rise up against us in judgment will be exposed and cast down. We pray for the manifold wisdom of God to rest upon all who are in authority over our country. May truth and discernment guide every decision they make in their public and private lives. Remove the unrighteous who are ruling. We cry for justice and mercy, truth and righteousness to be established. [See Prov. 21:1-2; Isa. 54:17; Rom. 8:26-31; 16:20; Eph. 3:10; 6:10-20; 1 Tim. 2:1-4.]

Guard our nation, dear Lord—our borders, our military bases, all educational facilities, public office buildings, stadiums, our ports, ship channels, bridges, postal system, all transportation systems (airlines, trains, busses, autos), water conduits, electrical and nuclear energy plants, gas/oil distribution centers, hospital and medical facilities, space center and research facilities, homes, and law enforcement services (add others as the Lord shows you).

Praise You, Lord
We enter Your gates with thanksgiving and Your courts with praise. Lord, we give thanks to You and praise Your name. For, Lord, You are good and Your love endures forever; Your faithfulness continues through all generations. You are enthroned over our nation through the praises of Your people. Praise and glory and wisdom and thanks and honor and power and strength be to our God for ever and ever. Amen. [See Pss. 100:4-5; 22:3, Rev. 7:12.]

Promises
Thank You, Lord, for Your promise that You will fulfill Your purpose for me and my family and You will not abandon the works of Your hands. [See Ps. 138:8.]

Salvation for Those Who Don't Know Jesus
God, it is not Your will that any should perish but that all come to repentance [see 2 Pet. 3:9]. *Therefore, I pray, "God, grant [name of person] repentance leading to the knowledge of the truth and grant that [name] may come to his [or her] senses and escape from the snare of the devil, having been held captive by him to do his will"* [see 2 Tim. 2:25b-26].

190

Times of Trouble

With the psalmist we cry out: "Then they cried to the Lord in their trouble. . . . He brought them out of darkness and the deepest gloom and broke away their chains" [Ps. 107:13-14]. We stand on Your Word and ask You to do this for us as we, Your children, cry out in trouble and distress. Please, Lord, rescue us and break down gates of bronze and cut through bars of iron. Save us. You stilled the storm and guided Your people to their desired haven, so we thank You in advance that You will do it for us. With the psalmist we too give thanks to You, Lord, for Your unfailing love and blessings and for lifting us from affliction. [See Ps. 107:15-41.] (You can personalize this with the names of those you are praying for.)

Terrorism

Lord, let any terrorist schemes against our nation and cities be exposed and stopped—absolutely thwarted before they can be carried out. Help those who guard our borders and are charged with keeping the nation safe to do their job with diligence and watchfulness.

Youth

Give the youth of our nation hearts to follow You, Lord—to live godly lives and to fulfill Your purposes for them. Turn the hearts of fathers to the children and hearts of children to their fathers in a loving way. Forgive us where we have failed. Raise up a generation of young people who will do great exploits for You. [See Dan. 11:32; Mal. 4:6.]

Endnotes

Chapter 1: But I Never Wanted to Be in a Battle!

1. "Most American Christians Do Not Believe That Satan or the Holy Spirit Exist," *Barna Group,* April 10, 2009. http://www.barna.org/barna-update/article/12-faithspiritual ity/260 (accessed July 8, 2009).
2. C. S. Lewis, *The Screwtape Letters* (New York: Macmillan, 1961), p. 3.
3. Herbert Lockyer, *All the Women of the Bible* (Grand Rapids, MI: Zondervan Books, 1958), p. 41.
4. This story is adapted from Quin Sherrer and Ruthanne Garlock, *Lord, I Need Your Healing Power* (Lake Mary, FL: Charisma House, 2006), pp. 3-4.

Chapter 2: Who Is the Enemy, and What Does He Want from Me?

1. R. Arthur Mathews, *Born for Battle* (Robesonia, PA: OMP Books, 2008), p. 28.
2. Dean Sherman, *Spiritual Warfare for Every Christian: How to Live in Victory and Retake the Land* (Seattle, WA: Frontline Communications, 1990), p. 82.
3. Ibid., pp. 83-84.
4. McCandlish Phillips, *The Bible, the Supernatural, and the Jews* (New York: World Publishing, 1970), p. 73.
5. Edith Schaeffer, *A Way of Seeing* (Old Tappan, NJ: Fleming H. Revell Co., 1977), p. 110.
6. Richard D. Dobbins, "Caring for the Casualties," *Charisma* (September 1990), p. 96.
7. William Gurnall, *The Christian in Complete Armour*, vol. 1, abridged by Ruthanne Garlock, et. al. (Carlisle, PA: Banner of Truth Trust, 1986), p. 54.

Chapter 3: What Our Spiritual Wardrobe Should Look Like

1. William Gurnall, *The Christian in Complete Armour*, vol. 1, abridged by Ruthanne Garlock, et. al. (Carlisle, PA: Banner of Truth Trust, 1986), pp. 66, 68.
2. Ibid., vol. 2, pp. 22-23.
3. W. E. Vine, *Vine's Expository Dictionary of Old and New Testament Words*, vol. 3 (Old Tappan, NJ: Fleming H. Revell, 1981), pp. 298-99.
4. Gurnall, *The Christian in Complete Armour*, vol. 2, p. 160.
5. Rick Renner, *Sparkling Gems from the Greek: 365 Greek Word Studies for Every Day of the Year to Sharpen Your Understanding of God's Word* (Tulsa, OK: Teach All Nations, 2003), pp. 156, 159.
6. Ibid., p. 159.
7. Gurnall, *The Christian in Complete Armour,* vol. 3, pp. 27-28, 30-31.
8. Dean Sherman, *Spiritual Warfare for Every Christian: How to Live in Victory and Retake the Land* (Seattle, WA: Frontline Communications, 1990), p. 45.
9. Vine, *Vine's Expository Dictionary*, vol. 4, p. 230.
10. R. Arthur Mathews, *Born for Battle* (Robesonia, PA: OMP Books, 2008), p. 16.
11. Ibid., p. 20.
12. Gurnall, *The Christian in Complete Armour*, vol. 3, p. 164.

Chapter 4: How Strong Can a Woman Be?

1. Associated Press, "Study: Moms Credited Most in Instilling Faith" [statistics by Search Institute of Minneapolis], *Florida Daily News*, February 10, 1990.
2. John Dawson, *Taking Our Cities for God: How to Break Spiritual Strongholds* (Lake Mary, FL: Creation House, 1989), pp. 27-29.
3. Judson Cornwall, *Praying the Scriptures: Communicating with God in His Own Words* (Lake Mary, FL: Creation House, 1990), pp. 212-13.

Chapter 5: The Disciplines of the Spirit-Empowered Woman

1. Finis Jennings Dake, *Dake's Annotated Reference Bible* (Lawrenceville, GA: Dake Bible Sales, Inc., 1963), p. 629. Other references given by Dake: Psalms 35:13; 69:10; 2 Samuel 12:16-23; Ezra 8:21; Matthew 4:1-11; 6:16-18; 9:15; Luke 5:33; Acts 9:7-9; 13:1-5; 1 Corinthians 7:5.
2. Arthur Wallis, *God's Chosen Fast: A Spiritual and Practical Guide to Fasting* (Fort Washington, PA: Christian Literature Crusade, 1968), pp. 41-42,86.
3. This story is from Gloria Phillips, *A Heart Set Free,* ed. Irene Burk Harrell (Wilson, NC: Star Books, 1985), pp. 39-41. Cry Aloud, the teaching ministry of Gloria Phillips, can be found on the Internet at http://www.gloriaphillipscryaloud.com.

Chapter 6: Our Weapons and Strategy

1. Paul E. Billheimer, *Destined to Overcome* (Minneapolis, MN: Bethany House, 1982), pp. 41,43.
2. Dean Sherman, *Spiritual Warfare for Every Christian: How to Live in Victory and Retake the Land* (Seattle, WA: Frontline Communications, 1990), p. 123.
3. H. A. Maxwell Whyte, *The Power of the Blood* (Springdale, PA: Whitaker House, 1973), p. 44.
4. Ibid., pp. 78-80,81.
5. R. Arthur Mathews, *Born for Battle* (Robesonia, PA: OMP Books, 1978), p. 66.
6. Ibid., p. 124.

Chapter 7: An Open Door to the Enemy

1. *The E. W. Bullinger Companion Bible* (Grand Rapids, MI: Zondervan, 1964), appendix 44, iv.
2. Other references concerning the sins of the fathers are Deuteronomy 29:24-28; 2 Chronicles 7:19-22; 34:23-25; Ezra 9:4,13-15; Nehemiah 9:1-3; Isaiah 65:6-7; Jeremiah 14:20-22; 16:10-13.
3. Burton Stokes and Lynn Lucas, *No Longer a Victim: Answers for the Pain Inside* (Shippensburg, PA: Destiny Image Publishers, 1988), p. 25.
4. Derek Prince, *Blessing or Curse: You Can Choose* (Old Tappan, NJ: Chosen Books, 1990), pp. 19, 145.
5. McCandlish Phillips, *The Bible, the Supernatural, and the Jews* (New York: World Publishing, 1970), pp. 75-76.
6. Herbert Lockyer, Sr., ed, *Nelson's Illustrated Bible Dictionary: An Authoritative One-Volume Reference Work on the Bible, with Full-Color Illustrations* (Nashville, TN: Thomas Nelson, 1986), p. 501.
7. Ed Murphy, "We Are at War," *Wrestling with Dark Angels: Toward a Deeper Understanding of the Supernatural Forces in Spiritual Warfare*, eds. C. Peter Wagner and F. Douglas Pennoyer (Ventura, CA: Regal Books, 1990), p. 60.
8. Ibid., pp. 68-71.

Chapter 8: Breaking Bondages

1. Archibald D. Hart, *Healing Life's Hidden Addictions: Overcoming the Closet Compulsions That Waste Your Time and Control Your Life* (Ann Arbor, MI: Servant Publications, 1990), p. 238.
2. We recommend Jan Frank's book, *Door of Hope* (Nashville, TN: Thomas Nelson, 1995), which provides steps toward recovery from abuse, based on her own experience as a victim of incest, and provides answers to common questions asked by abuse victims and those who seek to help them.
3. Statistics regarding the aftereffects of abortion, as well as helpful resources for post-abortion women, are available at http://www.afterabortion.org (sponsored by the Elliot Institute, P.O. Box 7348, Springfield, IL 62791-7348).

4. Excerpted from Anonymous, "One Woman's Walk through an Abortion Nightmare," *Charisma* (October 1990), pp. 96-108. Used by permission of the author.

Chapter 9: Fight for Your Children

1. Mel Gabler, "Have You Read Your Child's School Textbooks?" (Longview, TX: Educational Research Analysts). Mel Gabler's Educational Research Analysts website is located at http://www.textbookreviews.org.
2. David Barton, "Revisionsim: How to Identify It in Your Children's Textbooks," *Wall Builders*, January 2005. http://www.wallbuilders.com/libissuesarticles.asp?id=112 (accessed August 8, 2009).
3. Gregory R. Reid, *Trojan Church: The New Age Corruption of the Evangelical Faith* (Longwood, FL: Xulon Press, 2008), pp. 33, 48. Dr. Reid's (and Youth Fire's) Internet address is http://www.gregoryreid.com.
4. Greg Reid, *Teen Satanism: Redeeming the Devil's Children* (Columbus, GA: Quill Publications, 1990), p. 9.
5. George Barna, "Survey Describes the Ups and Downs of Tween Life," *Barna Group*, September 30, 2006. http://www.barna.org/barna-update/article/15-familykids/146-survey-describes-the-ups-and-downs-of-tween-life (accessed August 8, 2009).
6. Quin Sherrer and Ruthanne Garlock, *Praying Prodigals Home* (Ventura, CA: Regal, 2000), p. 28.

Chapter 10: Fight for Your Marriage

1. *Time*, "What Youth Think," *Women: The Road Ahead* (Fall 1990), p. 14.
2. James Dobson, *Love Must Be Tough: New Hope for Families in Crisis* (Waco, TX: Word Books, 1983), pp. 122-123.
3. Ibid., pp. 71-72.
4. Archibald D. Hart, *Children and Divorce: What to Expect, How to Help* (Dallas, TX: Word, Inc., 1982), pp. 34-35.
5. Bob Gass, "Tough Love," *The Word for You Today* (Third quarter, 2009), p. 34.
6. Hart, *Children and Divorce*, pp. 50-62.
7. Judy Reamer, *Feelings Women Rarely Share* (Springdale, PA: Whitaker House, 1987), pp. 89, 92, 145.

Chapter 11: Spiritual Healing and Warfare

1. Reginald Cherry, *Healing Prayer: God's Divine Intervention in Medicine, Faith and Prayer* (Nashville, TN: Thomas Nelson, 1999), pp. 116-117.
2. This story is from Arlene Strackbein, "Battle of the Mind," *Mighty Warrior* (Summer 1989), pp. 6-7,9. Used with permission.
3. Stanley Howard Frodsham, *Smith Wigglesworth, Apostle of Faith* (Springfield, MO: Gospel Publishing House, 2002), p. 111.
4. This story is from Gloria Phillips, *A Heart Set Free*, ed. Irene Burk Harrell (Wilson, NC: Star Books, 1985), adapted from pp. 192-196.

Chapter 13: Lessons from the Field

1. Adapted from Quin Sherrer and Ruthanne Garlock, *Lord, I Need to Pray with Power* (Lake Mary, FL: Charisma House, 2007), p. 7.
2. John Dawson, *Taking Our Cities for God: How to Break Spiritual Strongholds* (Lake Mary, FL: Creation House, 1989), p. 189.
3. Anne J. Townsend, *Prayer Without Pretending* (Chicago, IL: Moody Press, 1973), pp. 45-46.

Recommended Reading

Anderson, Neil T. *The Bondage Breaker*. Eugene, OR: Harvest House, 2000.

———. *Victory Over the Darkness*. Ventura, CA: Regal, 1990, 2000.

Billheimer, Paul E. *Destined to Overcome*. Minneapolis, MN: Bethany House, 2006.

Cornwall, Judson. *Praying the Scriptures: Communicating with God in His Own Words*. Lake Mary, FL: Creation House, 2008.

Dawson, John. *Taking Our Cities for God: How to Break Spiritual Strongholds*. Lake Mary, FL: Creation House, 2001.

Dobson, James. *Love Must Be Tough*. Carol Stream, IL: Tyndale, 2007.

Frank, Jan. *A Door of Hope*, rev. ed. Nashville, TN: Thomas Nelson, 1995.

Gurnall, William. *The Christian in Complete Armour*. Abridged by Ruthanne Garlock, et. al. 3 vols. Carlisle, PA: Banner of Truth Trust, 1986.

Hamon, Jane. *The Deborah Company: Becoming a Woman Who Makes a Difference*. Shippensburg, PA: Destiny Image, 2007.

Hart, Archibald D. *Healing Life's Hidden Addictions: Overcoming the Closet Compulsions That Waste Your Time and Control Your Life*. Ann Arbor, MI: Servant Publications, 1990.

Lewis, C. S. *The Screwtape Letters*. New York: HarperOne, 2001.

Mathews, R. Arthur. *Born for Battle*. Robesonia, PA: OMF Books, 2001.

Michaelson, Johanna. *Like Lambs to the Slaughter*. Eugene, OR: Harvest House Publishers, 1989.

Phillips, Gloria. *A Heart Set Free*. Edited by Irene Burke Harrell. Wilson, NC: Star Books, 1985.

Phillips, McCandlish. *The Bible, The Supernatural, and the Jews*. New York: World Publishing Co., 1970.

Prince, Derek. *Blessing or Curse: You Can Choose*. Grand Rapids, MI: Baker, 2006.

Reamer, Judy. *Feelings Women Rarely Share*, rev. ed. Springdale, PA: Whitaker House, 2003.

Reid, Greg. *Teen Satanism: Redeeming the Devil's Children*. Columbus, GA: Quill Publications, 1990. Available from Youthfire, P.O. Box 370006, El Paso, TX 79936.

Schaeffer, Edith. *A Way of Seeing*. Old Tappan, NJ: Fleming Revell, 1977.

Sheets, Dutch, *Authority in Prayer: Praying with Power and Purpose*. Minneapolis, MN: Bethany House, 2006.

———. *Intercessory Prayer: How God Can Use Your Prayers to Move Heaven and Earth*. Ventura, CA: Regal, 1996.

———. *Watchman Prayer*. Ventura, CA: Regal, 2000.

Sherman, Dean. *Spiritual Warfare for Every Christian*. Seattle, WA: Frontline Communications, 1992.

Sherrer, Quin ,and Ruthanne Garlock. *The Beginners Guide to Receiving the Holy Spirit*. Ventura, CA: Regal, 2002.

———. *Grandma, I Need Your Prayers: Blessing Your Grandchildren Through the Power of Prayer*. Grand Rapids, MI: Zondervan, 2002.

———. *Lord, Help Me Break This Habit: You Can Be Free from Doing the Things You Hate*. Grand Rapids, MI: Chosen Books, 2009.

———. *Lord, I Need to Pray with Power*. Lake Mary, FL: Charisma House, 2007.

———. *Lord, I Need Your Healing Power*. Lake Mary, FL: Charisma House, 2006.

———. *Praying Prodigals Home*. Ventura, CA: Regal, 2000.

———. *The Spiritual Warrior's Prayer Guide*, 2nd ed. Ventura, CA: Regal Publishing, 2010.

Smith, Alice. *Delivering the Captives: Overcoming the Strongman and Finding Victory in Christ*. Minneapolis, MN: Bethany House, 2006.

Stokes, Burton, and Lynn Lucas. *No Longer a Victim: Answers for the Pain Inside*. Edited by Betty Stokes. Shippensburg, PA: Destiny Image Publishers, 1988.

Wagner, C. Peter. *Praying with Power: How to Pray Effectively and Hear Clearly from God*. Shippensburg, PA: Destiny Image, 2008.

Wagner, C. Peter, and F. Douglas Pennoyer, eds., *Wrestling with Dark Angels*. Ventura, CA: Regal Books, 1990.

Wallis, Arthur. *God's Chosen Fast: A Spiritual and Practical Guide to Fasting*. Fort Washington, PA: Christian Literature Crusade, 1968.

White, Thomas B. *The Believer's Guide to Spiritual Warfare: Wising Up to Satan's Influence in Your World*. Ann Arbor, MI: Servant Publications, 1990.

Wright, Linda Raney. *Spiritual Warfare and Evangelism*. Crestline, CA: Linda Raney Wright.

About the Authors

Quin Sherrer has written or co-authored 28 books (primarily with Ruthanne Garlock) including bestsellers *A Woman's Guide to Spiritual Warfare, How to Pray for Your Children* and *Miracles Happen When You Pray.*

She has spoken to audiences in 40 states and 12 nations, encouraging them in their daily and sometimes challenging walks of faith. As a guest on more than 300 radio and television programs—including *The 700 Club, 100 Huntley Street* and various shows on the Daystar Television Network and the Trinity Broadcasting Network—she's addressed topics of prayer, hospitality, miracles and personal renewal.

Quin holds a B.S. degree in journalism from Florida State University. She spent her early career writing for newspapers and magazines in the Cape Kennedy, Florida, area where her late husband, LeRoy, was a NASA engineer. A winner of *Guideposts* magazine's writing contest, she also was named Writer of the Year at the Florida Writers in Touch Conference.

Quin now lives in Niceville, Florida, and serves on the leadership team of the Northwest Florida Area Aglow. She has three children and six grandchildren. You can contact Quin at the following:

P. O. Box 1661
Niceville, FL 32588
www.quinsherrer.com

Ruthanne Garlock is a Bible teacher and author with a varied background in international ministry to 35 nations. She has co-authored (with Quin Sherrer) 19 books on prayer and related subjects. Their book *God Be with Us: A Daily Guide to Praying for Our Nation* was nominated for the 2002 Gold Medallion Award in the devotional category by the ECPA.

For four years she and her husband, John, served with Continental Theological Seminary in Brussels, Belgium, and then for 23 years lived in Dallas, Texas, where John was an instructor at Christ For The Nations Institute and Ruthanne worked as a freelance writer and teacher. Since John's death in 2003, Ruthanne continues traveling and teaching on prayer and spiritual warfare at seminars, churches and women's groups.

Ruthanne holds a degree in Bible and religious education from Central Bible College, Springfield, Missouri, and is now living in the Texas Hill Country near San Antonio. She has three children and four grandchildren. You can contact Ruthanne at the following:

Ruthanne Garlock
P. O. Box 53
Bulverde, TX 78163
www.garlockministries.org

Books by Quin Sherrer
and Ruthanne Garlock

Becoming a Spirit-Led Mom

The Beginners Guide to Receiving the Holy Spirit

God Be with Us: A Daily Guide to Praying for Our Nation (finalist for
Gold Medallion Award, devotional category, 2002)

*Grandma, I Need Your Prayers: Blessing Your Grandchildren
Through the Power of Prayer*

How to Forgive Your Children

How to Pray for Family and Friends

How to Pray for Your Children

*Lord, Help Me Break This Habit: You Can Be Free from
Doing the Things You Hate*

Lord, I Need to Pray with Power

Lord, I Need Your Healing Power

The Making of a Spiritual Warrior: A Woman's Guide to Daily Victory

Prayer Partnerships: Experiencing the Power of Agreement

Prayers Women Pray: Intimate Moments with God

Praying Prodigals Home: Taking Back What the Enemy Has Stolen

The Spiritual Warrior's Prayer Guide

A Woman's Guide to Breaking Bondages

A Woman's Guide to Getting Through Tough Times

A Woman's Guide to Spirit-Filled Living

A Woman's Guide to Spiritual Warfare

Books by Quin Sherrer

Good Night, Lord: Inspiration for the End of the Day

A House of Many Blessings: The Joy of Christian Hospitality
(with Laura Watson)

How to Pray for Your Children

Listen, God Is Speaking to You: True Stories of His Love and Guidance

Miracles Happen When You Pray:
True Stories of the Remarkable Power of Prayer

Prayers from a Grandmother's Heart

The Warm and Welcome Home

Books by Ruthanne Garlock

Before We Kill and Eat You: Tales of Faith in the Face of Certain Death
(with H. B. Garlock)

Fire in His Bones: The Story of Benson Idahosa—
A Leader of the Christian Awakening in Africa

Books Contributed to by Quin Sherrer and Ruthanne Garlock

The Grandmother's Bible

Women of Destiny Bible: Women Mentoring Women
Through the Scriptures

Also by Quin Sherrer & Ruthanne Garlock

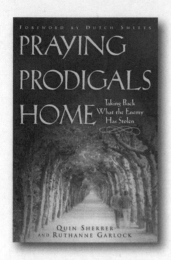

Praying Prodigals Home
Take Back What the Enemy Has Stolen
Trade Paper · ISBN 978-08307-2563-2

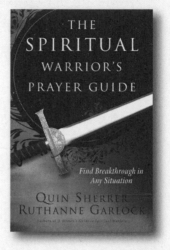

The Spiritual Warrior's Prayer Guide
Find Breakthrough in Any Situation
Trade Paper · ISBN 978-08307-4712-2

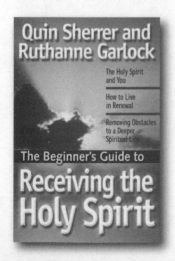

**The Beginner's Guide to
Receiving the Holy Spirit**
Trade Paper · ISBN 978-08307-3393-4

Available at
Bookstores
Everywhere!

Regal
God's Word for Your World™

www.regalbooks.com